HER KEYS TO THE CITY

HONOURING THE WOMEN WHO MADE DUBLIN

LORD MAYOR ALISON GILLILAND
AND CLODAGH FINN

Comhairle Cathrach
Bhaile Átha Cliath
Dublin City Council

First published in 2022 by
Dublin City Council
c/o Dublin City Library & Archive
139-144 Pearse Street
Dublin 2

A catalogue record is available for this book
from the British Library.

ISBN 978-1-8384635-5-7

Designed by Mark Dignam, KnockoutGraphics@gmail.com
Printed by Anglo Printers, Drogheda, Co Louth

Distributed by Four Courts Press
7 Malpas St, The Liberties, Dublin 8, D08 YD81

On the cover
Top row, from left:
Máirín Hope, Christine Buckley,
Pat Crowley, Speranza, Nan Joyce,
Agnes Bernelle in 'Salome'.
Bottom line, from left:
: Ethna Gaffney, Máire Molly Gill
and Eavan Boland

Acknowledgements

The first 'thank you' in this collection must go to the general public who nominated the women they thought deserved to be included in this book during a public consultation held in February 2022. While we could not include all suggestions, the vast majority have been included and allowed us a truly representative selection from among the often under-celebrated contributions of women throughout the decades. If a single theme unites all entries, it is the determination shown by these women to overcome obstacles to make Dublin, and in turn Ireland, a better place.

In the same way, the people involved in putting together this publication in just five months showed real determination and dedication to showcasing some of the city's remarkable women. The project was conceived as part of my priority as Lord Mayor to enhance the visibility of women. Thank you to everyone at the Lord Mayor's office and, in particular, to Fanchea Gibson who gives us a fascinating insight into the life of her predecessor Mary O'Sullivan in her illuminating entry.

This book would not have been possible without the dedication, commitment and expertise of journalist and author Clodagh Finn. From our first meeting, she has worked tirelessly with me to research, compile, write, edit, advise and project manage the realisation of this very special publication. She epitomises the determination and passion for her work so often shown by the women featured in this book – thank you, Clodagh, from the bottom of my heart!

Warmest thanks also to journalist and editor Rowena Walsh who did sterling work bringing so many of these women so beautifully to life. A special note of thanks to Holly Christine Callaghan whose enthusiasm and championing of strong women shine through her beautiful illustrations.

Many thanks, too, to Dublin City Council, Dublin City Library and Archive, and Deputy City Librarian Brendan Teeling. Under the library's auspices, this publication has also benefitted enormously from the expertise, input and unsparing help of historians Dr Mary Muldowney and Maeve Casserly. Very many thanks to other expert contributors, historian Mícheál Ó Doibhilín, author Eleanor Fitzsimons and art historian Dr Margarita Cappock.

It has been particularly special to include the contributions of family and friends who have offered us unmatched insights into the life and work of their loved ones. Heartfelt thanks to Dr Phyllis Gaffney, Leah Leslie, Iseult O'Malley, Catherine and Grace O'Malley, Prof Jonathan Wright, Dr Derval Conroy, Sarah Barnes, Sarah Binchy, Donal Buckley, Simon Ross and Dr John M. Rochford. Family members and friends also offered information, anecdotes and photographs. Thank you Jacqui Deevy, Dr Sarah Fitzgibbon and Barbara Fitzgibbon, Síobhra Aiken, Heather Laskey, Audrey Conlon, Gail Slater, Jennie Ryan, Phyl Herbert, Gay Murphy, Tim McDonnell, Robert Coyle, Amy Long, Rosa Meehan, Ruth O'Herlihy, Lee Dillon, Lorraine and Christy Cahill, Sophie Sassi-Gorman, the Crowley family, Joan O'Connor, Carole Pollard, Sandra O'Connell of the Royal Institute of the Architects in Ireland, Margaret McEvoy, Wendy Barrett and Susan Early, Peter Hanly, Dr Conor Heffernan, and Mary Kennedy and Mary McDaid of the Fitness League Ireland.

The list goes on to include those who provided photographs at the shortest notice, among them Alan Hayes, Arlen House, Dr Una Kealy, Waterford Institute of Technology, Dr Brian Dolan, Rob Twamley, Tony Maxwell, Conor McCabe, Conor Doyle and Patrick Purcell, Vera Klute, Nicola Kelly, OPW-Maynooth University Archive and Research Centre, Emma Keogh and Ciarán Cooney at RTÉ Archives, UCD Archives, Trinity College Dublin, the Royal Irish Academy, the Royal College of Physicians in Ireland, Irish Military Archives, the Hugh Lane Gallery, the Sybil Connolly Collection at the Hunt Museum, the National Library of Ireland, the Irish Photo Archive, the Abbey Theatre Archive, Dublin Institute for Advanced Studies, the Irish Labour History Society, Noreen Maher, Rosita Sweetman, Máirín de Burca, Mary Kenny, Alan Kinsella, Sinéad Guckian, Fórsa trade union, the Irish League of Credit Unions, John Reidy, Eoghan Doyle, Youth Theatre Ireland, Holocaust Education Trust Ireland, the Irish Jewish Museum, Pavee Point, King's Inn, Cormac O Culáin at the Law Library, Kunak McGann, The O'Brien Press, David Conachy, Sunday Independent, the Irish Architectural Archive, Boston College John J. Burns Library, Ros Kavanagh, Phyllis Breslin, Sheila Wallace, Cliona Plunkett and Mick O'Farrell.

A special thank you, too, to Brenda Fitzsimons, picture editor at the Irish Times, Cormac Bourke, editor of the Irish Independent and Tom Fitzpatrick, editor of the Irish Examiner for their help with photographs and permissions.

Kate Nevin and Dr Sinéad McCoole of the wonderful website mna100.ie went out of their way to help locate photographs and secure permissions, as did photographer Derek Speirs. It was very much appreciated.

There were many interested helpers who proofread, fact-checked or simply cheered us on. Thank you Nuala Finn, Ciara Finn, Margaret Jennings, Grainne Cunningham, Deirdre McElligott, Dr Emer O'Beirne, Claire Kerr, Douglas Smith, Dr Ida Milne, Dr Mary McAuliffe, Liz Gillis, Historian in Residence, South Dublin County Council, Dr Margaret Ward and Lucy Keaveney, co-founder of the Countess Markievicz School.

In compiling this book, myriad sources – archives, books, interviews, newspapers, to mention a few – were used. We have decided not to list all of them as Her Keys to the City is intended as an easy-to-read introduction to some of the women who shaped our history. While every possible effort was made to get every fact and detail correct, we apologise for any errors or omissions and would be very happy to receive clarifications at the Lord Mayor's office. In the same way, if a reader is interested in a particular reference, please get in contact.

We also received a generous response for images. We can't thank you enough for your help. Any source that we have not mentioned here is credited under the gratefully received images. Every possible effort was made to trace copyright holders and to get their permission.

Finally, a very special mention for designer Mark Dignam, a person of endless patience and boundless creativity. An enormous thank you, too, to Padraic Kierans of Anglo Printers who brought this book into being in the flash of an eye.

We hope, however, that this volume will act as an introduction to further seeking and more story-telling. It's up to you now to continue the story.

Contributors

Clodagh Finn

Clodagh Finn is a journalist and author of *Through Her Eyes: a new history of Ireland in 21 women* and *A Time to Risk All* (Gill Books), a biography of Mary Elmes, the 'Irish Oskar Schindler'. She is an *Irish Examiner* columnist who has worked as a sub-editor and feature writer for several newspapers, and as a freelance writer and editor in Paris. She has a degree in French and Archaeology from UCD and is particularly interested in writing about overlooked women from history. **CF**

Rowena Walsh

Rowena Walsh is a journalist, editor and communications consultant. She has worked as an editor in the features department of the Irish Independent and as a feature writer for the *Irish Independent* and *Irish Examiner*. She holds an MA in European Economic and Public Affairs and a BA in History and Politics, both from UCD. **RW**

Dr Mary Muldowney

Dr Mary Muldowney is the Dublin City Council Historian in Residence for Dublin Central. She has published widely in a variety of media, making history as accessible as possible to academic and general audiences. She has a particular interest in labour and women's history, often using oral history interviews as her primary source. Mary is a member of the Expert Working Group of the Grangegorman Histories project. She is also a member of the organising committee of the Irish Labour History Society and is a co-editor of Saothar, the Society's internationally recognised journal. **MM**

Maeve Casserly

Maeve Casserly is a Fulbright Creative Ireland Museums Scholar. She has an MPhil in Public History and Cultural Heritage from Trinity College Dublin and is completing an MLitt in University College Dublin. She is a heritage practitioner in the National Library of Ireland and her most recent publication is 'Exhibiting Éire: representations of women in the centenary commemorations of the Easter Rising,' in (ed.) Oona Frawley *Women and the Decade of Centenaries* (2021). She was Historian in Residence for Dublin City South East. **MC**

Holly Christine Callaghan

Holly Christine Callaghan is an illustrator and visual artist. Her work has included lead illustrator on three animated films and documentaries. She enjoys a balance of commercial design work and bringing her own studio creations to exhibitions, which often feature strong women in history. All illustrations in the book are by Holly unless otherwise stated. **hollyartist.com**

There are a number of family members, friends or experts in their fields who very kindly contributed single profiles. They are named in each entry.

Foreword

Lord Mayor Alison Gilliland

The awarding of the Freedom of the City of Dublin, which began in 1876, acknowledges people who have made a significant contribution to our city. Of the 83 Freedoms of the City awarded and subsequently included on the Roll of Honour, only four have been given to women at the time of writing.*

Margaret Sandhurst, who campaigned for votes for women, was awarded the Freedom of the City in 1889, along with her husband James. Beloved entertainer Maureen Potter was honoured in 1984; the Crown Princess of Japan Michiko, along with her husband the then Crown Prince of Japan, Akihito, in 1985 and, finally, in 1993, Mother Teresa.

While Aung San Suu Kyi was awarded the Freedom in 2000, she was subsequently removed from the Roll of Honour in 2017. Michelle Obama, along with her husband Barack, was awarded the Freedom in 2016, but she has not yet signed the Roll of Honour.

The genesis of this book lies in wanting, in some way, to address this very obvious gender imbalance and to showcase a variety of the very many accomplished women who lived before us. Collectively, these women were central to major social and political changes in our country's history, excelled across diverse disciplines and realised major achievements in many different fields.

Each left us with an important legacy and were influential role models in their day. Indeed, many continue to be role models for us today. You will be familiar with some of the women featured, but many others are not that well known outside their immediate work circle.

So you'll meet some very interesting women as you read through this book – a book that, I hope, gives them all the keys of acknowledgement to our city.

*Following my proposal in May to Dublin City Council, three more women will be awarded the Freedom of the City in June 2022. They are social justice activist Ailbhe Smyth, cyber-psychologist Professor Mary Aiken and Olympian Kellie Harrington.

Contents

Anne Devlin

(1780-1851)

Nationalist and heroine

For 48 years, Anne Devlin defied the might of Dublin Castle, resisting its threats, bribes, torture and the destruction of her family, which had been successfully farming in Co Wicklow when she was born in 1780. She was a happy child, in a happy family.

But her life changed in 1798 with the United Irish Rebellion. Her cousins Michael Dwyer and Arthur Devlin were being hunted after that, and Anne would visit their hideouts in the Wicklow mountains.

Her father Bryan was arrested on the word of a paid informer and kept in Wicklow Gaol without trial for almost three years. On his release, he moved his family to Rathfarnham in Dublin for safety.

It was there that Anne met Robert Emmet on his return from Europe as he sought a suitable house in which he could plan a rebellion. Anne volunteered to pose as his (unpaid) housekeeper, meeting all who visited the house and plotted with Emmet. Often, he discussed his plans with her, and he

Anne Devlin illustration by Holly Christine Callaghan

1

A commemorative stamp issued in 2003 illustrated by Holly Christine Callaghan

The garret in which Anne died illustrated by Micheál Ó Doibhilín

Anne in her prison cell illustrated by Micheál Ó Doibhilín

would not interrupt discussions with others when she entered the room. He described her as "one of our own".

Anne delivered his messages and knew all Emmet's depots in Dublin. On the day of his rebellion – 23 July 1803 – she acted as second-in-command, co-ordinating the distribution of weapons, ammunition and explosives as well as messages from his house until he returned, defeated and dejected.

Emmet fled into the mountains, but Anne remained. When yeomen arrived looking for him, she said she "knew nothing".

They half-hanged her, stabbed her with bayonets, to no avail.

The Devlin family was arrested and brought to Dublin Castle. There, Anne met Town Major Sirr who offered her the then immense sum of £500 for the names of those involved with Emmet, but she refused to tell him and was sent with her family to Kilmainham Gaol.

There, she met Dr Edward Trevor, effectively controller of the Gaol. Anxious to gain the reward offered for Emmet's fellow conspirators, he attempted to get their names from Anne. He tried psychological torture, sensory deprivation, starvation, solitary confinement, threats and promises, but not even the death of her youngest brother could break her.

When she was eventually released, in 1806, she was almost on her death bed, having contracted the skin condition erysipelas from the filthy conditions.

Anne recovered while working as a lady's companion to Mrs Hanlon until her employer died in 1810, The next year, Anne married drayman William Campbell; a "good man", she claimed. Together, they had four children. She took in washing from the wealthy to augment William's income.

Everywhere Anne went she was followed by a policeman, unobtrusively at first, to identify those she might talk to. Later, he was in uniform, to frighten everyone away, effectively keeping Anne in solitary confinement in an open prison until her death.

William died in 1846, just as the Famine was beginning to affect accommodation and food prices in Dublin. Suffering from rheumatism, and frequently blinded by recurring bouts of erysipelas, she could not work and was forced to move to Dublin's worst slum – Little Elbow Lane. Her son William tried to help her, and occasionally paid her 6d rent when he had work. But he was frequently sick and, in fact, the day before she died, Anne was seen nursing him in her garret. Having pawned the last of her clothes three days before to buy a small loaf of bread, she died on 18 September, 1851.

At any time over the previous 48 years, Anne could have turned to that policeman and offered the names of 50 people who had assisted Emmet and achieve immense wealth. Because she did not – despite her desperate need – they remained at large, able to safely inspire and educate others.

Thanks to her, a woman who put her country's freedom ahead of herself, Emmet's spirit remained alive until, eventually, Ireland was free, in his words, to "take her place among the nations... as an independent country".

Mícheál Ó Doibhilín, historian, public speaker and publisher

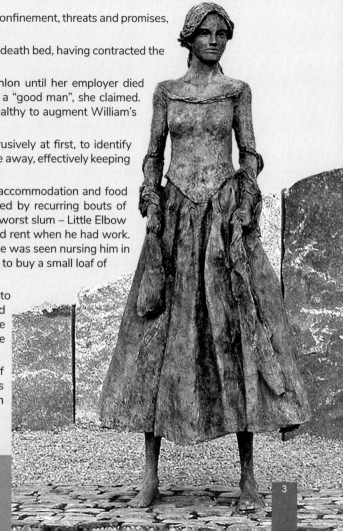

A statue of Anne Devlin by sculptor Clodagh Emoe in Rathfarnham, Co Dublin. Picture courtesy of www.kilmainhamtales.ie

Speranza/Jane, Lady Wilde

(1821-1896)

Poet, writer, nationalist and mother of Oscar

Jane Elgee, best known as Speranza, was born into a staunchly unionist family on 27 December 1821. Her childhood was turbulent and her education haphazard, but she studied voraciously and mastered several languages. Ireland's troubled history sparked her patriotic zeal. "Once I had caught the national spirit, all the literature of Irish wrongs and sufferings had an enthralling interest for me," she declared.

During her early 20s, she submitted revolutionary poetry that documented the twin tragedies of famine and forced emigration to *The Nation*, weekly newspaper of the Young Ireland movement. Editor Charles Gavan Duffy was astonished to discover that "John Fanshaw Ellis" his brilliant new contributor, was "the spirit of Irish liberty embodied in a stately and beautiful woman".

Jane adopted the name Speranza, Italian for hope. She also accepted commissions to translate books from German, Latin and French. Novelist William Carleton described her as, "the most extraordinary prodigy of a female that this country, or perhaps any other, has ever produced".

Illustration of Speranza by Holly Christine Callaghan

Cover and frontispiece of Ancient Legends of Ireland

On 12 November 1851, Speranza married Dr William Wilde, who she described as "a celebrity – a man eminent in his profession, of acute intellect and much learning, the best conversationalist in our metropolis, and author of many books, literary and scientific". Her uncle insisted: "Had she married a man of inferior mind he would have dwindled down into insignificance or their struggle for superiority would have been terrific."

They had three children: Willie, Oscar and Isola. In January 1864, William was knighted in recognition of his services to the medical profession and his role in compiling census statistics. Speranza became Lady Wilde without hesitation. She hosted weekly conversaziones and supper parties in their fine home at 1 Merrion Square North. When *Poems by Speranza* was published in 1864, she dedicated it: "To Willie and Oscar: I made them indeed, speak plain the word COUNTRY. I taught them, no doubt, that a country's a thing men should die for at need!"

The *Boston Pilot* noted: "How her indignation blazes forth at the coolness with which the loss of a million of her countrymen is taken".

Hard times followed. Speranza lost a scandalous libel case taken by a young patient of her husband's. Their daughter, Isola, died shortly before her tenth birthday. When William

JANE LADY WILDE
'SPERANZA'
1821–1896

File, Scríbhneoir, Gníomhaí
A CHÓNAIGH ANSEO

Poet, Writer, Activist
LIVED HERE

Commemorative plaque at Jane's home in Merrion Square

Oscar's success delighted her, and she succumbed to profound melancholy when he was imprisoned. By then, she was struggling financially, living in fear of the bailiffs.

On 3 February 1896, Speranza, Lady Wilde, aged 74, died of "acute bronchitis". She was eulogised in *The Freeman's Journal* as, "almost the last of that brilliant circle of poets and writers who, fifty years ago, gave to the 'Young Ireland' movement a world-wide celebrity".

The *Virginia Enterprise* described her as "a brilliant woman who had contributed much to literature and social life in England and Ireland".

Eleanor Fitzsimons, author of *Wilde's Women: How Oscar Wilde Was Shaped by the Women He Knew* (Duckworth Books Ltd)

This entry is based on Eleanor's address at the unveiling of a Dublin City Council commemorative plaque (inset) at 1 Merrion Square on 19 November 2021

WORKS BY LADY WILDE.

Driftwood from Scandinavia.

Sidonia the Sorceress. From the German.

"Eritis Sicut Deus;" or, The First Tempta-
tion. From the German. 3 vols.

The Glacier Land. From Dumas.

The Wanderer and His Home. From Lamartine.

Pictures from the First French Revolution.

The Future Life. Swedenborg.

Poems, &c., &c.

died, Speranza lost her lovely Dublin home. She joined her sons in London, where she established herself as an essayist for leading publications. Her topics were always serious. "I can't write," she declared, "about such things as 'Mrs Green looked very well in black, and Mrs Black looked very well in green'".

In *The Bondage of Women*, she raged: "For six thousand years, the history of women has been a mournful record of helpless resignation to social prejudice and legal tyranny". Her ebullience restored, she revived her Saturday salon.

Anne Jellicoe

(1823-1880)

Founder of Alexandra College, pioneer of women's education and social reformer

When Anne Jellicoe founded Alexandra College at Earlsfort Terrace, Dublin, in 1866, there were just six full-time students on the roll. Under her guidance as lady superintendent – and with help from Church of Ireland Archbishop Richard Chenevix-Trench – the college flourished and opened the way for women to gain access to higher education.

The college was the first institution of its kind in Ireland and it offered women a wide-ranging curriculum that included English and literature, science, history, Latin, music, drawing and callisthenics.

Anne Jellicoe also campaigned to extend public exams to include girls' schools and she lived long enough to see the introduction of the Intermediate Education Act in 1878. Alexandra College students not only sat the examination's three grades – junior, middle and senior – but won prizes.

While boys still significantly outnumbered girls in the early years, the new legislation helped to chip away at attitudes among a public still reluctant to give women access to higher education.

Anne Jellicoe, pioneering educationalist and social reformer
Illustration by Holly Christine Callaghan

Elliott & Fry, ALEXANDRA COLLEGE, DUBLIN. London, W.

Picture courtesy of Dublin City Library and Archive

Shortly before she died on 18 October 1880, Anne Jellicoe said: "The success of the College is my ample reward."

That college is testament to Anne Jellicoe's determination to provide advanced education to young women at a time when there were no real academic opportunities, but it is just one achievement in a lifetime devoted to improving the lives of women.

Anne Jellicoe was born into a Quaker home in Mountmellick, Co Laois, in 1823, to William Mullin, a Quaker schoolmaster and his wife Margaret. Her only sibling, a brother John William, probably went to her father's school, but she was most likely educated by a governess.

In 1846, she married John Jellicoe, a Quaker miller

From the Cork Examiner, 1963

The Anne Jellicoe commemorative plaque at Buswells Hotel in Dublin

and the couple moved to Clara, Co Offaly, where she set up an embroidery factory to give jobs to local women. It gave her an insight into the working conditions of women, an interest that heightened when she and her husband moved to Harold's Cross, Dublin, a decade later.

She got deeply involved in the social life of the city. She supported a Quaker-run infant school on Meath Street and wrote about the harsh conditions women faced in factories and as prisoners in Mountjoy prison. She saw education as a way of improving women's lives. Before she set up Alexandra College to focus on a more academic, university-type learning for women, she along with fellow educationalist Barbara 'Ada' Corlett, founded a society that would become the Queen's Institute for the Training and Employment of Educated Women in 1861 in Dublin.

It was the first technical college of its kind in Ireland or indeed in the UK and it trained women in bookkeeping, telegraphy, lithography and wood-engraving, to name a few. Women now had the education necessary to sit Royal Dublin Society exams and qualify with commercial certificates.

The first Civil Service jobs for women as telegraph clerks went to its graduates in 1870.

The Freeman's Journal described the Institute as "one of the most practically useful established in Ireland", though the economic depression of the 1880s forced its closure in 1882.

Nonetheless, in her lifetime Anne Jellicoe made an exceptional contribution as a pioneering educationalist and a social reformer. She investigated conditions in factories and in prisons, established vocational training courses for women and founded a college that played a pivotal role in reforming education for women in the 19th century.

Many of its past-pupils – from trade unionists Louie Bennett (see entry on Louie Bennett) and Helen Chenevix (see entry on Helen Chenevix) to illustrator and republican Grace Gifford – went on to shape a new Ireland. Alexandra College continues to prosper today.

CF

Anna Maria Haslam

(1829-1922)

Women's rights campaigner, social reformer and co-founder of the Dublin Women's Suffrage Association

Anna Maria Haslam is best-known as a women's rights campaigner, but she was a true Renaissance woman with a deep interest in all aspects of the world around her. The list of her interests and countless endeavours are testament to that.

She was involved in temperance, anti-slavery and pacifist societies. She was a member of the Rathmines Literary Society, the Fresh Air Society (which brought poor city children into the countryside) and the Irish Society for the Prevention of Cruelty to Children, to mention a few.

She promoted women's education, practiced homeopathy and wrote several newspapers articles in which she was "forceful and adroit in her argument", to quote *The Freeman's Journal*.

Anna Maria Haslam was also the family breadwinner, running a stationery and toy shop in Rathmines, Dublin, when ill health forced her husband Thomas Haslam to stop working in 1866. She supported the two of them – there were no children – for the next three decades, but still found time to campaign on a range of issues.

Anna Maria Haslam. Picture public domain

'When she died, the Freeman's Journal noted that "there passed away one of the most remarkable characters who figured in the public life of Dublin for the last quarter of a century"'

Portrait of Thomas and Anna Maria Haslam by Sarah Cecilia Harrison in 1908. Picture courtesy of the Hugh Lane Gallery

If there was a single issue that dominated her life, it was women's suffrage, and her interest in that started young. As a young girl, she read – and was influenced by – such writers as Maria Edgeworth, novelist and essayist, and Harriet Martineau, considered the UK's first female sociologist.

Born into a Quaker family in April 1829 in Youghal, Co Cork, Anna Maria was the 17th of Abraham and Jane Fisher's 18 children. She was educated in Quaker schools, in Waterford and later in Yorkshire, England, and married Thomas Haslam in 1854. He was a fellow Quaker and supporter of women's rights. The couple moved to Dublin in 1858 where they both actively promoted women's suffrage.

Anna Maria would later say that one of the most memorable events in her life was taking part in a women's suffrage march in London in 1860. A decade later, she was at the head of a similar procession in London and was organising meetings in Dublin.

In 1876, with her husband, she founded the Dublin Women's Suffrage Association which later became the Irish Women's

Commemorative bench in St. Stephen's Green

Suffrage and Local Government Association. As its secretary, she helped to organise meetings, fundraise, shape public opinion by writing letters to the newspapers and give a platform to high-profile speakers, such as Belfast journalist and feminist Isabella Tod.

Both she and Tod campaigned for the repeal of the Contagious Diseases Acts of 1864 which imposed a double sexual standard by allowing the arrest of prostitutes who were subjected to an examination for venereal disease. Men, however, went free. The acts were repealed in 1886.

While Anna Maria was a staunch campaigner for women's rights, she opposed all physical force and once labelled women who used it to further their aims as "vociferous vixens". She remained a Unionist all of her life. She was a member of the Women's Liberal Unionist Association, as she believed social reform was more likely within the union than under home rule.

She cast her first vote in 1918, when women over 30 were granted the right to vote. On polling day, and 89-year-old Anna Maria was paraded to the booth by elated members of radical and moderate suffrage groups, demonstrating her important and influential role in the many years of struggle to attain the franchise.

When she died four years later, *The Freeman's Journal* noted that "there passed away one of the most remarkable characters who figured in the public life of Dublin for the last quarter of a century".

The following year, sculptor Albert Power set Anna and Thomas Haslam's contribution in stone with a limestone bench in St Stephen's Green, Dublin, honouring "their long years of public service chiefly devoted to the enfranchisement of women".

CF/MC

Pictures courtesy of Dublin City Library and Archive

Anna Maria Haslam was a staunch campaigner for women's rights, but she opposed all physical force

THE CAMERON STUDIO, 70, MORTIMER ST., REGENT STREET.

Alice Stopford Green

(1847-1929)

Writer and nationalist who shaped Irish history during the early years of the State

Alice Stopford Green was "the most important Irish writer of the day", according to one reviewer. It was 1911 and the renowned historian's second book on Irish history had been published. Her first *The Making of Ireland and Its Undoing* was a deliberately controversial look at the country in medieval times, which sought to contradict the contemporary English belief that Ireland lacked an indigenous civilisation.

At the time, Alice was living in London. Widowed after the death of her husband John Richard Green in 1883, she devoted her mornings to work, starting at 5am. After noon, her home was a meeting place for those in political, social and literary circles, including Oliver Wendell Holmes, Florence Nightingale and Henry James.

Later, her circle would include champions of Ireland's cultural revival such as Jack Yeats, John O'Leary and the German scholar Kuno Meyer.

Alice Sophia Amelia Stopford was born on 30 May, 1847, in Kells, Co Meath, the seventh of Edward and Anne's nine

Alice Stopford Green. Picture public domain

children. She was widely read and helped her father with his work as archdeacon of Meath.

After Edward's death in 1874, the family moved to England, where she met her husband. Green, a pioneering social historian, had published what would become a seminal work – *A Short History of the English People* – and the couple collaborated on *A Short Geography of the British Islands*.

When John died after five years of marriage, Alice completed his *Conquest of England*. A scholar in her own right, she became a member of the Royal Historical Society.

'Her first book The Making of Ireland and Its Undoing' was a deliberately controversial look at the country in medieval times, which sought to contradict the contemporary English belief that Ireland lacked an indigenous civilisation.'

Always interested in Ireland, Alice's views evolved as she studied the impact of British colonialism in Africa. She investigated the treatment of prisoners held on the south Atlantic island of St Helena during the Boer War and became a founding member of the Africa Society.

She began to consider how Irish history had been presented, and examined commercial, industrial and education elements of the late-medieval and early modern period in *The Making of Ireland and Its Undoing*.

Although Alice wrote on Irish history for the rest of her career, her involvement in the struggle for Irish nationalism extended beyond pen and paper.

Alice presented the Senate with a jewelled casket containing a vellum scroll with the signatures of those who sat in the first Senate.

She and Roger Casement had met when the Congo Reform Association was established in 1904. She later hosted Casement, Eoin MacNeil and Erskine Childers in her London home and helped to raise money to fund arms for the Irish Volunteers.

Despite her involvement in the 1914 Howth gun-running, Alice did not believe in armed rebellion and was shocked at the events of Easter 1916. Still loyal to Roger Casement who would be executed for his part in the uprising, she campaigned for his reprieve.

In 1918, she moved from London to Dublin. Her house at St Stephen's Green became a meeting place for nationalists during the War of Independence and was often raided by British forces.

A supporter of the Anglo-Irish Treaty, she joined Cumann na Saoirse and was nominated to the Free State Senate as one of four women members.

In 1924, she presented that chamber with a jewelled casket containing a vellum scroll with the signatures of those who sat in the first Senate. The Senate Casket was given to the Royal Irish Academy in 1936.

Alice died on 28 May, 1929. Her grave marker displays the accolade: "Historian of the Irish People".

RW

The frontispiece of Alice's 1920 publication
'The Making of Ireland and Its Undoing'

THE
MAKING OF IRELAND
AND ITS UNDOING

1200-1600

BY
ALICE STOPFORD GREEN

MAUNSEL AND COMPANY, LTD.
DUBLIN AND LONDON. 1920

Margaret Lindsay Huggins

(1848-1915)

Pioneering astronomer who, with her husband William, laid the foundations for astrophysics

Together, Margaret Murray and William Huggins had "one of the most successful husband-and-wife partnerships in the whole of astronomy," according to fellow astronomer J. B. Hearnshaw.

The description, in his book *The Analysis of Starlight: One Hundred and Fifty Years of Astronomical Spectroscopy*, is certainly apt as the couple's home was also their place of work and their 30-year scientific collaboration led to many discoveries in the field of spectroscopy.

When William was named a Knight Commander of the Order of the Bath during Queen Victoria's diamond jubilee year, Margaret – or Lady Margaret as she became – was included in his 1897 citation. It read: "For the great contributions which, with the collaboration of his gifted wife, he had made to the new science of astrophysics". Margaret was unique because, with the exception of the Queen, she was the only woman whose name appeared on the honours list.

Margaret, born in Dublin on 14 August 1848, was the eldest

Margaret Lindsay Huggins
illustration by Holly Christine Callaghan

Margaret Huggins' Observatory

child of John Majoribanks Murray and his wife Helen, who died in 1857. She spent her childhood and early adulthood in Monkstown, Dublin. She was educated privately at home, where she studied art, classics, literature and music. Her paternal grandfather Robert Murray encouraged her fascination with the stars and taught her to recognise the constellations.

She read works by the mathematician and astronomer John Herschel and the Irish scientific writer Dionysius Lardner, studied sunspots using a terrestrial telescope and experimented with photography.

Meanwhile, William was working in the new field of astronomical spectroscopy – the study of matter through its interaction with light fields (electromagnetic radiation) – when he met Margaret. She was already an admirer of his work when they were introduced by Irish telescope maker Howard Grubb in Dublin in 1873.

The couple married in Monkstown Parish Church two years later, when Margaret was 27 and William was 51. She moved to Tulse Hill in south-west London, where William had a private observatory, and they embarked on a decades-long collaboration by becoming the first to take the dry gelatine photographic plate, which had caused a revolution in photography, and applying it to astronomical spectroscopy.

They studied the spectra of planets, photographed the spectrum of Tebbutt's comet and, in 1889, Margaret was cited as 'co-author' with her husband when their paper *On the Spectrum, Visible and Photographed*, of the great *nebula in Orion* was published.

The following year, Margaret and William won the Actonian Prize of the Royal Institution for their work *An Atlas of Representative Stellar Spectra*. She was also elected to the council of the recently established British Astronomical Society.

While Margaret was admitted to the Royal Astronomical Society as an honorary member in 1903, women would not receive the same status as men – full membership – until over a decade later.

Margaret and William's final published research, inspired by meeting Marie and Pierre Curie, focused on methods of observing radioactive radiation spectroscopically.

Margaret also found time to contribute to *Observatory* magazine and *Encyclopaedia Britannica*. Her varied interests included art and music and she published a monograph on the 16th-century violin maker Gio Paolo Maggini.

In 1909, the couple collaborated on the *Collected Scientific Papers of Sir William Huggins*. When her husband died the next year, Margaret began working on his biography.

A keen advocate of women's education, she donated scientific and personal papers to Wellesley College, a private women's college in the United States. Margaret knew the founding director of the college's observatory.

She was 66 when she died on 24 March 1915. Two years later, Margaret's scientific brilliance was recognised when a memorial to the couple was unveiled in St Paul's Cathedral in London. She was described as her husband's 'fellow worker'; an indelible reminder of her importance in their joint endeavours and achievements in astrophysics.

A commemorative plaque also celebrates her early years at her former home at 23 Longford Terrace in Monkstown, Co Dublin.

RW

Anna Parnell

(1852-1911)

Artist, writer, patriot and co-founder of the Ladies' Land League

Anna Parnell's contribution to the Irish Land War of the late 19th century was at least as significant as that of her more famous brother Charles Stewart, yet nearly eight decades would pass before her account of it, *The Tale of a Great Sham*, was published by Arlen House in 1986.

Written in 1907, it casts new light on the woman herself – hailed as an Irish 'Joan of Arc' in the 1880s – and it reveals the revolutionary vigour of the Ladies' Land League (LLL).

As leader of the League, Anna Parnell travelled around Ireland and spoke directly to women, urging them to take action by withholding rent and resisting eviction. "Learn to depend on yourselves and to do things for yourselves and organise yourselves," she told them.

Her energetic management of the League was so effective that Ellen Ford, writing in the *Irish World* newspaper, proclaimed: "Great indeed is the power of this young girl, whose slightest suggestion a nation will obey! A very Joan of Arc is she."

Anna and her older siblings Charles Stewart (1846-1891)

'Learn to depend on yourselves and to do things for yourselves and organise yourselves'
Illustration of Anna Parnell by Holly Christine Callaghan

19

Dr Margaret Ward, historian, and Lucy Keaveney, co-founder of the Countess Markievicz School, who both worked to bring Anna Parnell's work and achievements back into the light, at the unveiling of a plaque at the former headquarters of the Ladies' Land League by the Lord Mayor Alison Gilliland. Picture courtesy of Damien Eagers

and Fanny (1848-1882) were considered the political ones among the 11 children born to Anglo-Irish landowner John Henry Parnell and his American wife Delia Tudor at Avondale House in Co Wicklow. When Anna was seven her father died and the family moved to Dublin.

Perhaps because her mother was American, Anna had more exposure to the world than was usual for a woman at the time. At 18, she enrolled in the School of Art of the Royal Dublin Society. She later studied in London and spoke several languages – French, German, Italian and Russian.

She and her sister Fanny were in America when famine again swept through the west of Ireland in 1879. The sisters worked for the Famine Relief Committee and set up 25 branches with about 5,000 members in America, paving the way for women's involvement in politics.

When Anna moved back to Ireland in 1881, she was asked to take over the reins of the Irish Land League while the male leaders were in prison. It was considered a "most dangerous experiment". It proved to be just that as the women succeeded in doing something that the men had failed to do; they established a militant force to challenge landlord rule.

By 1882, there were 500 branches of the Ladies' Land League, with several hundred members in each.

In May of that year, under the Kilmainham Treaty, Charles Stewart Parnell and all prisoners were released on the condition that Parnell used his influence to quell rural agitation.

Initially, the male leaders were happy to allow the women continue their work, but only if they could control it. Anna Parnell was furious, saying the women would be no more "than perpetual petticoat screens behind which the men could shelter". She felt the men had settled for too little. For her, full Irish independence was the only desirable outcome.

There were acrimonious negotiations and the LLL was dissolved that August. Anna never spoke to her brother again. She was also plunged into deep grief following the sudden death of her sister Fanny, aged 33, the previous July. Anna Parnell moved to north Devon where she lived under an assumed name until she died by drowning in 1911.

On the 110th anniversary of her death, a plaque honouring her contribution was unveiled at the former headquarters of the LLL on O'Connell Street in Dublin. Now, a campaign to repatriate her remains from a graveyard in Devon to Glasnevin cemetery is gathering pace.

CF

The Ladies' Land League executive. Their contribution to the Irish Land War of the late 19th century was significant. Photo: Public domain

Katharine Tynan

(1859-1931)

Poet, novelist and leading light of the Irish Revival

In the words of writer George Russell, Katharine Tynan was "the earliest singer in that awakening of our imagination which has been spoken of as the Irish Renaissance".

For WB Yeats too, who described her as an "Irish Christina Rossetti", her poetry played a key part in the Irish literary movement. He edited her writing, was a major influence on her work and may have even proposed to her, but their deep friendship was finally sundered when she sold their correspondence for £100 in 1920.

Katharine, who was a nationalist and a Parnellite, believed that "affection for England and love of Ireland could quite well go hand in hand". Columnist Kevin Myers once described her as belonging to a species which has no visible expression today, "a Home Rule Unionist, a Loyal Separatist, a woman and artist who cherished her Irishness, and longed for self-government, but felt herself comfortable within the United Kingdom".

She was born on 23 January 1859 in South Richmond Street in Dublin, the fifth of 12 children of Elizabeth and Andrew Tynan.

Katharine Tynan. Picture public domain

From 1868, she was brought up in the family home, White Hall in Clondalkin in Co Dublin, where visitors included such notables as Charles Stewart Parnell, Michael Davitt, Douglas Hyde, JM Synge and Russell.

She was educated at the Dominican Convent of St Catherine of Siena in Drogheda, where she developed her love for the works of Dickens and Thackeray. She began writing at a young age, despite suffering from eye ulcers which left her severely myopic. Her first published piece Dreamland appeared in Young Ireland in 1875.

Later, her poems were published in several magazines including Graphic, Irish Monthly, Hibernia and Dublin University Review. She became acquainted with the Jesuit Father Matthew Russell, an avid supporter. When she later moved to London, Father Russell introduced her to his brother Sir Charles Russell. It was at the latter's house where she met Oscar Wilde, who employed her as a contributor to the magazine he was editing, The Women's World.

A selection of publications from Katharine's vast body of work

Katharine was also a prolific novelist, writing 102 books throughout her career. Her popularity was ascribed to her ability to tell an interesting story, and the humanity of her characters.

Henry was appointed as resident magistrate for Castlebar in Co Mayo in 1911, and the family moved back to Ireland, settling in Claremorris. By this time, she had had two sons, Toby and Pat, and a daughter Pamela, who would later become an acclaimed writer.

Her sons enlisted to fight in the First World War, Pat on the frontline in France, while Toby went to Palestine. Both survived the fighting. During the War, she wrote to soldiers and their families and kept a detailed diary of the early years of the conflict. She did not support the Easter Rising, referring to it as a "rebellion".

In 1885, she met WB Yeats, the same year her first poetry collection was published. He described her style in *Louise de la Vallière and Other Poems* as being "too English". Katharine took note. *Shamrocks*, which was published two years later, had a strongly Irish slant.

She married Henry Hinkson, a Dublin-born lawyer and writer, in London on 4 May 1893. She moved to that city, where she embarked on a dynamic career as a freelance journalist. Interested in social justice, she focused on the treatment of shop girls, unmarried mothers, infanticide, capital punishment and the education of the poor.

After her husband's death in 1919, Katharine left Ireland and returned to England, although she travelled extensively, referring to this period as her wandering years. She kept writing and her final novel, *The Playground*, was published in 1930. She died on 2 April 1931 in London.

A major contributor to the Irish Literary Revival, Katharine's poem *The Wind That Shakes the Barley* was turned into a popular folk song, which is still sung today.

RW

Prof Mary Hayden

(1862-1942)

First female professor of Irish history and feminist

Mary Hayden was born in Dublin in 1862. She was one of the first women to study for a degree when the Royal University (now University College Dublin) was established. While women were admitted, they did not have access to teaching by the university fellows, who were all appointed to men's colleges.

Mary graduated with a BA in modern languages in 1885, a year after the first degrees were conferred on women. She got an MA in 1887 and, in 1895, she was one of the first two women to win the Royal University Junior fellowship.

Enjoying the cultural life of late 19th-century Dublin, she mixed with many of its leading figures. Unlike her friend Hanna Sheehy-Skeffington, however, she had little interest in Irish politics. She disapproved of the 1916 Rising and was a constitutional nationalist, rejecting violence.

Mary kept a diary for more than two decades and her observations offer a fascinating window on her early life, her hopes, achievements and disappointments. None of her private papers from the later part of her life seem to have survived.

Prof Mary Hayden. Picture courtesy of Alan Hayes

Mary Hayden, 1900. Picture courtesy of Alan Hayes

She first became active when she campaigned for the admission of women to teaching and other facilities of the universities. In 1902, she was a founding member and vice-president of the Irish Association of Women Graduates and Candidate Graduates. Their efforts were largely responsible for the inclusion of women in the 1908 legislation that established the National University of Ireland and its constituent colleges.

Recognising her academic credentials, University College Dublin appointed her to the foundation staff, and in 1911 she became the first holder of the professorship of modern Irish history. She was also appointed to the governing body of the college and to the senate of the National University of Ireland (NUI).

The work for which Mary was most widely remembered was *A Short History of the Irish People*, co-authored with George Moonan in 1921. The book was still being used in teaching 20 years after Mary's death in 1942.

She continued to pursue political causes, remaining a member of the senate of the NUI until 1924. In the 1930s, she represented the National Council of Women in Ireland and the NUI Women Graduates Association in their protests against reactionary economic and social government policies. Her last major public campaign, aged 75, was to oppose articles 40, 41 and 45 in the 1937 Constitution, which were seen as relegating women to a domestic role.

After the text of the new Constitution was published, Mary reversed her lifelong non-party-political stance and proposed that all women graduates meet to discuss the document's possible threats to the status of women. That meeting, which

> '*Her last major public campaign, aged 75, was to oppose articles 40, 41 and 45 in the 1937 Constitution, which were seen as relegating women to a domestic role*'

the press noted was very well-attended, unanimously agreed to call for the deletion of the problematic articles. It also called for a reinsertion of earlier measures guaranteeing equality.

Mary went on to help form the Women's Social and Progressive League as a political party committed to opposing the Constitution and any regressive consequences it would entail.

She received an honorary doctorate from the NUI in 1935, three years before she retired. She spoke Irish, Greek and Hindustani fluently. She travelled widely, especially in her earlier years, spending a lot of time in Greece and India, where she also learned Sanskrit. In her spare time, she cycled and swam, even learning to dive at 70, according to one account. She also dedicated her time in retirement to helping improve the welfare of Dublin children. She died on 12 July 1942 in Rathmines, Dublin.

MM

Mary helped form the Women's Social and Progressive League as a political party committed to opposing the 1937 Constitution. Picture courtesy of Alan Hayes

The police disrupt a meeting of the Ladies' Land League in 1881

milestones

1878

The Intermediate Education Act grants female students the right to participate in public competitive examinations, take university degrees and enter careers and professions.

1881

Women take the reins of the Irish Land League in 1881 when the male leaders are imprisoned. It is considered a "most dangerous experiment". It proved to be just that because Anna Parnell, as head of the Ladies' Land League, did what the men thought impossible; she established a militant force to challenge landlord rule.

That year the police disrupted a women's meeting, but work continued until 1882 when the organisation was disbanded by Charles Stewart Parnell, as part of the Kilmainham Treaty. Anna never spoke to her brother again. *(See entry on Anna Parnell)*

1882

Married women are allowed a separate legal existence to that of their husband under The Married Women's Property Act.

1886

The Contagious Diseases Acts of 1864, 1866 and 1869 are repealed. Under the contentious acts, any woman suspected of being a prostitute could be arrested and subjected to an examination for venereal disease. *(See entry on Anna Maria Haslam)*

1893

A statue of Father Mathew, the temperance campaigner, is unveiled on O'Connell Street in Dublin. It was sculpted by Mary Redmond, from Tipperary, one of the few female sculptors of the time.

Sarah Cecilia Harrison

(1863-1941)

Artist, friend of the poor and first woman to sit on Dublin City Council

Sarah Cecilia Harrison was a compelling woman who broke new ground – as an artist, an activist, a suffragist and a city councillor. She came from a Northern Irish family steeped in politics, who supported Home Rule, so perhaps it was inevitable that on her move to Dublin in 1904, she would devote herself wholeheartedly to many different campaigns of a philanthropic, political and civic nature.

In tandem with these activities, Sarah established herself as a well-respected portrait painter in Dublin and was one of the staunchest supporters and closest allies of Sir Hugh Lane (1875-1915), the Irish art connoisseur, collector and dealer. She also supported his campaign for the establishment of a modern art gallery for Ireland. Sarah believed that an entitlement to employment, adequate housing and access to modern art for all were compatible aspirations. Her strikingly modern and enlightened approach was married with a strong degree of tenacity, pragmatism and a formidable work ethic.

For over three decades, she was a champion of the poor and

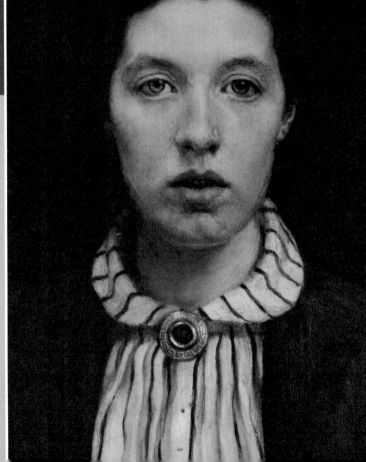

A self-portrait of Sarah Cecilia Harrison.
Picture courtesy of the Hugh Lane Gallery

Sarah's portrait of Sir Hugh Lane.
Picture courtesy of the Hugh Lane Gallery

the unemployed in Dublin. She was passionate about the rights of women and the needs of children and saw the tenement crisis as being at the root of many of the city's problems. As a feminist, she was one of the Irish suffrage movement's most prominent activists, breaking new ground when she became the first female councillor for Dublin Corporation in 1912. Sarah made a real difference to the lives of many marginalised citizens.

What is truly remarkable about her is that, first and foremost, she was a very talented artist, and she maintained a thriving portrait practice while achieving so much in other domains. Her early prowess as an artist was noted from her training at the Slade in London, where she was the recipient of a number of prizes. Sarah had a busy portrait practice in Dublin and painted portraits of many significant individuals.

The breadth of her achievements is astounding and if one wanders around Dublin city, the traces of her legacy are evident in a multitude of places. Her paintings hang in the Hugh Lane

31

Gallery, the National Gallery, the Royal College of Surgeons, the Law Library and City Hall. The Haslam memorial bench in St Stephen's Green was thanks to Sarah Cecilia Harrison who instigated a campaign to have a permanent memorial to the Haslams (see entry on Anna Maria Haslam) for their public service in the 'enfranchisement of women'.

Until recently, her contribution to the city of Dublin has been overlooked and forgotten, but she deserves to be reinstated to her rightful position as a significant political pioneer, an accomplished portraitist and a tireless campaigner. Sarah's work on behalf of Hugh Lane, both during his lifetime and following his untimely death when the RMS *Lusitania* was torpedoed and sunk in May 1915, was significant. She attended the opening of the gallery in its permanent home in Charlemont House, Parnell Square, in 1933.

She died on 23 July 1941 at the age of 78. Her tombstone in Mount Jerome cemetery in Dublin reads: 'Artist and Friend of the Poor' – a succinct epitaph for a woman who achieved so much in her life.

Dr Margarita Cappock, editor of *Sarah Cecilia Harrison: Artist, Social Campaigner, and City Councillor*, published by Dublin City Council

A self-portrait of Sarah Cecilia Harrison.
Picture courtesy of the Hugh Lane Gallery

Constance Georgine Markievicz

(1868-1927)

Republican, labour activist and first female Cabinet minister in Ireland (and second in Europe)

Constance Gore-Booth was born on 4 February 1868 at Buckingham Gate, London, and was brought at an early age to the family home at Lissadell, Co Sligo. In 1893, she went to the Slade School of Art in London.

On her return to Lissadell, she became involved in the women's suffrage movement. She remained interested in art, and her parents allowed her to go to Paris in 1898. There, she met fellow art student Count Casimir Dunin-Markievicz, a Pole whose family held land in the Ukraine. They married in London in 1900. Their daughter, Maeve, was born the next year. The couple returned to Paris in 1902, leaving their daughter in the care of Lady Gore-Booth. They separated amicably in 1909.

In the 1916 Easter Rising, Constance was second-in-command of a troop of ICA combatants at St Stephen's Green.

33

By 1911, Markievicz had become an executive member of Sinn Féin and Inghinidhe na hÉireann. She became an honorary treasurer of the Irish Citizen Army (ICA) which was founded in 1913. In the 1916 Easter Rising, Constance was second-in-command of a troop of ICA combatants at St Stephen's Green. As British troops occupied buildings surrounding the park, the ICA troop found refuge in the College of Surgeons. After a week of heavy fire, they surrendered.

'Markievicz was originally sentenced to death for her part in the rebellion, but this was commuted because of her sex'

Markievicz was originally sentenced to death for her part in the rebellion, but this was commuted because of her sex. She was transferred to Aylesbury prison and was released under a general amnesty in June 1917.

Markievicz was one of the many advanced nationalists imprisoned in 1918 on account of their alleged involvement in the so-called 'German plot'. She was invited to stand as a Sinn Féin candidate for Dublin's St Patrick's division in the general election of December 1918. She was the first woman to be elected to the British parliament, but like all Sinn Féin MPs she refused to take her seat at Westminster. On her release and return to Ireland in March 1919, she was named Minister for Labour in Dáil Éireann.

A Call to :: the Women of Ireland

BY
Constance de Markievicz

DUBLIN:
Published by Fergus O'Connor
1918

PRICE - SIXPENCE

A portrait of Countess Constance Markievicz by Boleslaw von Szankowski in 1901. Picture courtesy of the Hugh Lane Gallery

Picture courtesy of Dublin City Library and Archive

After the War of Independence, Markievicz refused to take her seat in the Dáil because of her opposition to the terms of the Anglo-Irish Treaty. She was again forced to go into hiding while former comrades became embroiled in the Civil War. She wrote anti-Treaty articles and engaged in speaking tours to publicise the republican cause.

Elected to the Dáil for Dublin South in August 1923, she refused to take the oath of allegiance to the king and, like other elected republicans, she thus disqualified herself from sitting. She was arrested for the last time in November 1923 while attempting to collect signatures for a petition for the release of republican prisoners, and went on hunger strike until she and her fellow prisoners were released just before Christmas.

During the last decade of her life, Constance Markievicz spent time in Kilmainham Gaol, Cork Gaol and Mountjoy Gaol in Ireland. She was also imprisoned for a time in Aylesbury Gaol and Holloway Gaol in England. She wrote frequently to her sister Eva, who became her greatest support. *The Prison Letters of Countess Markievicz* were first published in 1934 and have since come to be regarded as a classic of feminist literature, as well as shedding light on the political beliefs of a key figure in the Irish revolutionary period.

Markievicz joined Fianna Fáil when it was established in 1926, breaking her ties with Cumann na mBan, which opposed the new political party. She stood successfully as a Fianna Fáil candidate for Dublin South at the June 1927 general election, but her health was failing. She died on 15 July 1927 and was buried in Glasnevin cemetery.

MM

Eva Gore-Booth, poet, and her elder sister Constance

Louisa 'Louie' Bennett

(1870-1956)

Novelist, pacifist, women's rights activist and trade union leader

When Louisa, or Louie as she was known, Bennett was first asked to help reorganise the trade union movement at a Trade Union Congress in Sligo in 1916, she had "absolutely no idea how to go about it", she told the *Irish Press* in an interview many years later.

"But," she went on, "I was burning with enthusiasm. I had no money. No office. No furniture. Nothing. But I went out and I got one member to start me off. I put her name down in a twopenny jotter and hoped fervently for more."

Two years later, membership of the Irish Women Workers' Union (IWWU) had increased to over 5,000. In the decades that followed, the union won several improvements in pay and conditions for women, most notably, in the laundry strike of 1945 when it organised a three-month stoppage by 1,500 workers.

At one point, Louie noted that "the attitude of the employers would make Bolsheviks of us all" such was their reluctance to make any concessions. Laundry workers often worked 13-

Louie Bennett. Picture from the *Irish Press*, 1955

LOUIE BENNETT (1870-1956) SUFFRAGETTE, TRADE UNIONIST.

Commemorative stamp issued to honour Louie

hour days in conditions that caused "great fatigue, excessive perspiration and blistered feet". At least they received some pay, unlike the thousands of Irish women in Magdalene laundries who worked, effectively as slaves, for nothing.

The strike was successful and it won the right to two weeks' paid annual holidays which benefitted all workers.

However, Louie Bennett might never have entered the trade union movement. She initially wanted to be a novelist and wrote two well-reviewed, though commercially unsuccessful, novels. The Spectator review of The Proving of Priscilla (1902) was largely positive: "Slightly crude, but exceedingly clever and arresting, is Miss Bennett's story of Priscilla, the charming maiden of Puritan ideals who marries a man of the world, and runs her head against all the stone walls of society."

Her second novel A Prisoner of his Word (1908) was described as "a pleasant, exciting romance written in a vigorous and nervous style".

Louisa 'Louie' Bennett was born into a prosperous Protestant,

Unionist family, the eldest of auctioneer James Cavendish Bennett and his wife Susan's children. She had a privileged education, studying at Alexandra College in Dublin, then at a young ladies' academy in London and later in Bonn, Germany, where she studied singing.

She became politically active around 1910 and, with her life-long partner Helen Chenevix, co-founded the Irishwomen's Suffrage Federation which established links with other organisations in Europe and the United States.

Throughout her life, Louie Bennett stressed the need for women to come together internationally if they wanted to make progress. "Women should remember that, despite

St. Stephen's Green bench dedicated to Louie and her life-long partner Helen Chenevix

went to the US to speak out about Black and Tan atrocities and worked as a mediator in the Civil War.

She remained active until her retirement aged 85. Then, she told journalist Ann Daly that she hoped to spend it in the garden or write a book about trade unionism and women.

She died the following year in 1956. She and her life-long partner Helen Chenevix are commemorated for their work in fighting for women's rights on a bench in St Stephen's Green in Dublin.

CF

the progress we have made, they still must, unfortunately, fight to hold their corner. And they can't do that by huddling together and thinking of themselves alone. They must organise with women all over the world. That is their weapon. That is their strength," she said in 1955.

She spent much of her own life trying to unite women to bring about change. She worked in the soup kitchens during the 1913 Lockout in Dublin and raised money to help the families of locked-out workers. She gave public-speaking classes to members of the Irish Women's Franchise League, but she was firmly against any form of militant violence.

She was deeply affected by the murder of Francis Sheehy-Skeffington, writer, activist and editor of the *Irish Citizen*, in 1916. She had worked with him on the paper, correcting proofs. Later in 1920, she

Photograph by courtesy]   *[Evening Ma*

Louie Bennett speaking at an Annual Convention of the I.W.W.U.;
Miss Catherine Keegan, *President*; and Mrs. Margaret Buckley.

Dr Kathleen Lynn

(1874-1955)

Medical practitioner, politician and republican nationalist

Dr Kathleen Lynn was an influential politician and activist, as well as an innovative medical doctor. She was born in 1874 in Killala, Co Mayo, to Robert Lynn and Katherine Wynne. Her father was a Church of Ireland clergyman and their family settled in Cong, Co Mayo, in 1886. Growing up in the west of Ireland in the aftermath of the Famine, Kathleen witnessed the diseases suffered by the local people because of their difficult living conditions, and this influenced her decision to become a doctor.

In 1891, she enrolled in Alexandra College in Milltown, Dublin and then studied at the Royal University of Ireland (now University College Dublin). From 1897, Kathleen attended Cecilia Street's school of medicine and the Royal College of Surgeons.

Following her graduation, she completed postgraduate work in the United States, before returning to Dublin to work at hospitals in the city. In 1903, she established a private general practice at 9 Belgrave Road, Rathmines, Dublin, her home until her death in 1955. She was appointed a fellow of the Royal College of Physicians in 1909.

Dr Kathleen Lynn. Picture courtesy of
Royal College of Physicians in Ireland

STANDING COMMITTEE · SINN FEIN · 14TH ARD FHEIS · DUBLIN · FEB. 21, 1922.

Kathleen (seated third from left) in the Sinn Féin 1922 Standing Committee. Also pictured are Kathleen Clarke, Jennie Wyse Power and Hanna Sheehy-Skeffington. Picture courtesy of the National Library of Ireland

Kathleen was a supporter of the women's suffrage movement and a member of moderate and militant organisations. In 1912, she tended imprisoned suffragettes on hunger strike. Her work among the poor led her to support social reforms and, in 1917, she was appointed vice-president of the Irish Women Workers' Union.

She was influenced by labour activists such as Countess Markievicz and James Connolly, and often attributed her politicisation to the actress, nationalist and labour activist Helena Molony, who had stayed at her home following an illness in 1913. Kathleen joined the Irish Citizen Army (ICA), at James Connolly's invitation, where she taught first aid to Cumann na mBan and the ICA. During the 1913 Dublin Lockout, she worked as ICA medical officer in Liberty Hall providing food and care to destitute families.

As chief medical officer of the ICA during the 1916 Easter Rising, she tended to the wounded from her post at City Hall. As second in command, Kathleen took full leadership of her garrison after Séan Connolly was killed. After their surrender, Kathleen was detained in Richmond Barracks and Kilmainham Gaol.

Kathleen was a prominent politician and was elected vice-president of the Sinn Féin Executive in 1917 and 1923, and successfully ran at local and general elections. Her home in Rathmines with Madeleine ffrench-Mullen (see entry on Madeleine ffrench-Mullen), whom she lived with since 1915, was a meeting point for fellow Sinn Féin women. It was notably used for meetings of Cumann na dTeachtaire (League of Women Delegates) which sought greater representation from women within Sinn Féin.

Kathleen was arrested and held in Arbour Hill in October 1918. But, following the intervention of the Lord Mayor of Dublin, Laurence O'Neill, the authorities agreed to release her because her medical services were indispensable during the influenza epidemic.

Her medical career was defined by her work at St Ultan's Children's Hospital. In May 1919, Kathleen established this

Receipt for the Dr Lynn Memorial Fund for Julia Grenan and Elizabeth O'Farrell. Picture courtesy of the National Library of Ireland

Dr Kathleen Lynn on rounds in St Ultan's Hospital. Picture courtesy of the National Library of Ireland

groundbreaking institution with Madeleine ffrench-Mullen and a group of social and political activists. It was the first hospital dedicated to paediatric care in Ireland. The environment of St Ultan's, headed by prominent figures in medicine and women's suffrage, encouraged its staff to be innovators.

Ultan's, named after Ultan of Ardbraccan, patron saint of paediatricians, opened at 37 Charlemont Street with £70 and two sleeping cots. Kathleen's ongoing work with Dublin's inner-city poor convinced her of the necessity for a hospital to provide medical and educational facilities for impoverished mothers and infants.

Under the leadership of Dr Lynn, the ethos of the hospital was patient-orientated. Ultan's grew rapidly, and from 1937 became a centre for the BCG vaccination programme against tuberculosis in Ireland.

In her medical practice, Kathleen expounded the virtues of fresh air and the outdoors, which she also applied to her own life. The architect Michael Scott, a personal friend, designed an outdoor balcony for her bedroom, where she slept for most of the year. She died in St Mary's Nursing Home in Ballsbridge in 1955 and was buried in Deansgrange cemetery with full military honours.

After her death, her cottage in Glenmalure in the Wicklow Mountains was given to An Óige, a youth hostel association she had worked with.

MC

Cissie Cahalan

(1876-1948)

Suffragette and trade unionist who led a successful strike for better pay and conditions

In 1906, Cissie Cahalan worked as a draper's assistant in Arnott's of Henry Street, Dublin. Micheal O'Lehane, the founder and general secretary of the Irish Drapery Assistants Association (IDAA), organised a meeting in the Rotunda Meeting Rooms to campaign for an end to the living-in system. At this time, shop assistants generally lived in the premises, and often they were locked in overnight by their employers. Their living conditions were frequently overcrowded and unhealthy. O'Lehane testified to a parliamentary inquiry in 1908 that 300 workers in Arnott's were living on the premises.

Cissie joined the union and soon became an active shop steward in the department store.

The struggle for women's suffrage was becoming more militant in the first decade of the 20th century and Cissie, who was born in Cork in 1876, joined the Irish Women's Franchise League (IWFL), which had been founded in 1908 by Hanna and Francis Sheehy-Skeffington and others. She was one of the few working-class members of the IWFL. Her feminist

From a postcard in the ICTU collection

Masthead for *The Irish Citizen*

THE IRISH
CITIZEN

For Men and Women Equally
The Rights of Citizenship;
From Men and Women Equally
The Duties of Citizenship.

Printed in
Ireland
on
Irish Paper.

Weekly
One Penny.
Annual
Subscription
6s. 6d. post free.

Vol. 4   DUBLIN, JUNE 12, 1915   No. 4

THE IRISH UNION OF DISTRIBUTIVE WORKERS AND CLERKS.

EXECUTIVE OFFICERS, 1922 AND 1923.

Cissie Cahalan, President of the Irish Union of Distributive Workers and Clerks, 1922-23. Picture courtesy of the Irish Labour History Society

instincts were honed by her work with the IDAA, in which she was a member of the Ladies Committee. The committee encouraged female members of the union to participate at all levels, not just the shop floor.

The range of her interests at this time is evident in the articles she wrote for the union journal. She described the lack of gender equality in the workplace, and at meetings of the suffrage movement she raised the difficulties facing working-class women. By 1912, she was a regular speaker at suffrage meetings. She also contributed to the *Irish Citizen*, the suffragist paper founded by Francis Sheehy-Skeffington and Francis Cousins.

'She played a vital role in organising the strike at Arnotts in which up to 450 workers secured a 30 per cent wage increase'

Cissie also wrote about the First World War and its particular impact on the poor, echoing the anti-war stance of both the IWFL and the Irish Congress of Trade Unions and Labour Party (ICTULP). The latter issued a widely distributed leaflet warning of the dire consequences for Irish people of involvement in the war, particularly in relation to shipping food produce out of the country.

Cissie was dismissed from Arnott's in 1916, possibly because of her campaigning work. However, by early 1917 she had been reemployed by the company, and in the period that followed, continued to juggle her work there with increasing commitment to political activity.

Elected to the committee of the IWFL from 1917-18 and the executive committee of the IDAA in April 1918, she played a vital role in organising the strike at Arnott's in which up to 450 workers secured a 30 per cent wage increase. She canvassed for Constance Markievicz in the general election of December 1918 and for female candidates in the 1920 local elections.

After the 1916 Rising, Louie Bennett (see entry on Louie Bennett) took over the leadership of the Irish Women Workers' Union (IWWU). Bennett believed that women needed an independent organisation to defend their interests, as many male members of the labour movement were reluctant to admit women to trade unions on an equal basis.

Cissie believed the opposite, arguing that women should involve themselves in the mixed unions and fight for power that way. The two women carried on the debate in the pages of the Irish Citizen for some years.

In December 1919, Cissie wrote: "I would remind Miss Bennett that the pioneers of the Suffrage did not seek to establish a separate parliament for women, but demanded a place in the nation's parliament. If women in the industrial world want a place in the labour movement, they must seek it in the Labour Parliament, shoulder to shoulder with the men and not in any separate organisation apart and isolated."

In April 1921, she was elected president of the union, which had now become the Irish Union of Distributive Workers and Clerks (IUDWC). During her term, she oversaw the establishment of a minimum wage and an end to the living-in system. She was elected to the national executive of the Irish Trade Union Congress (ITUC) in 1922 and 1923.

Cissie Cahalan died on 27 August 1948 in Dublin, and was buried beside her husband, John Wesley Burns (d. 1936), in Glasnevin cemetery.

MM

Arnotts poster from the 1911 Census online

Hanna Sheehy-Skeffington

(1877-1946)

International political and social activist, politician and suffragette

Hanna Sheehy-Skeffington worked energetically for women's suffrage, for equal rights and for Irish independence. Hanna (Johanna) Sheehy was born on 24 May 1877 in Kanturk, Co Cork, to David Sheehy, an Irish Parliamentary Party MP, and Elizabeth Sheehy. Part of the first generation of Irish women admitted to university on the same terms as men, she graduated with an honours BA in modern languages from the Royal University of Ireland (now University College Dublin) before receiving her MA in 1902.

Hanna met Francis Skeffington while they were studying, and they married in 1903 becoming the Sheehy-Skeffingtons. Their son, Owen, was born in 1908. The couple worked together on causes ranging from women's suffrage, to socialism, pacifism and Irish nationalism. Their equal partnership was unusual in this period, and they were sometimes subject to ridicule.

Hanna joined the Irish Women's Suffrage and Local Government Association (IWSLGA) led by Anna Haslam (see entry on Anna Maria Haslam) in 1902. Despite their political differences – Anna was a unionist and Hanna a nationalist –

1929 photo of Hanna (far left) with The International Peace Group, one of the peace and freedom organisations she was affiliated with. Picture courtesy of the National Library of Ireland

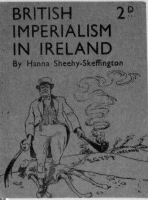

Cover of *British Imperialism in Ireland*, a pamphlet written by Hanna, first banned in Great Britain, giving an account of the death of Francis. Picture courtesy of the National Library of Ireland

Cartoon mocking the protest at Dublin Castle

they worked together often. By 1908, however, Hanna had become disillusioned with the IWSLGA's moderate approach and formed the radical Irish Women's Franchise League (IWFL) with Margaret Cousins.

This more militant group staged protests, which sometimes led to violence and arrests. In 1912, eight IWFL members, including Hanna, smashed the windows of government buildings to object to the lack of women's suffrage provisions in the new Home Rule Bill. Hanna was arrested and served two months in Mountjoy Prison. While imprisoned, she achieved political prisoner status and went on hunger strike to protest the treatment of two English suffragettes.

The *Irish Citizen* newspaper, founded by the Sheehy-Skeffingtons and Cousins in 1912 to promote IWFL campaigns, became the 'voice' of the Irish suffrage movement.

During the Easter Rising, Francis tried to organise civilian patrols to prevent looting. On 25 April, returning home, he was arrested by British soldiers and taken to Portobello Barracks. The following morning, Francis and two other civilians, Patrick McIntyre and Thomas Dickson, were shot without trial on Captain Bowen-Colthurst's orders. Bowen-Colthurst was court-martialled and found guilty, but insane.

IN HIGH SOCIETY.

At a recent Suffragette meeting in the Park the audience became so hostile and their attitude so threatening to some of the Suffragettes and their supporters had to seek refuge in the Zoological Gardens.

Mr. SHEEHY SKEFFINGTON (who may be easily recognised wearing his cycling suit)—"Th heavens, I've escaped from those barbarians."

This political cartoon satirises Francis's work for women's suffrage

Hanna felt the official inquiries into her husband's death were inadequate and refused offers of compensation. Instead, she decided to publicise the circumstances of Francis's death and, at the invitation of the Friends of Irish Freedom, undertook a tour of the United States from October 1916 to August 1918, speaking at over 250 meetings.

Hanna joined Sinn Féin in 1918. Her experiences of unequal treatment within the party informed her work with Cumann na dTeachtaire, a group which campaigned for greater female representation. Hanna was elected to Dublin Corporation in 1919 and became the Chair of the Public Libraries Committee. During the War of Independence, she was appointed as a judge in the republican courts and participated in the peace negotiations at Earlsfort Terrace.

In addition to her appointment as a Director of Organisation for Sinn Féin in 1921, she was elected to the 1922 Standing Committee, where she used her position to push for greater opportunities for women within the party.

Hanna took the anti-Treaty side when the Dáil split in 1922. She helped form the Women Prisoners' Defence League (WPDL) with prominent anti-Treatyites, such as Maud Gonne MacBride, to fundraise for the anti-Treaty side. In 1923, she travelled to Paris to persuade the League of Nations that it should not recognise the new Irish Free State, but she was unsuccessful.

Hanna continued her international activism after the Civil War as a member of the Women's International League for Peace and Freedom. She was secretary of the Friends of Soviet Russia, and in August 1930 visited Russia as part of a delegation. Hanna was appointed to the executive of Fianna Fáil in 1926, but split with the party when de Valera entered the Dáil. She campaigned vigorously against the 1937 Irish Constitution and helped establish the Women's Social and Progressive League.

Hanna Sheehy-Skeffington died in 1946 and was buried beside her husband Francis in Glasnevin cemetery.

MC

Dr Ella Webb

(1877-1946)

Pioneering paediatrician and co-founder of the Children's Sunshine Home (now LauraLynn)

During the 1916 Easter Rising, Dr Ella Webb cycled through gunfire to attend the temporary hospital she set up with "commendable promptitude", as the *Irish Times* put it, to treat the wounded from both sides of the conflict. It took her just three hours to get number 40 Merrion Square ready to receive 50 patients, the paper noted.

She had even set up an emergency operating theatre and, in her role as District Superintendent of the St John Ambulance Brigade, she enlisted the help of a few voluntary nurses who also travelled through firing lines to get medical equipment to tend the wounded.

Two years later, Dr Webb was awarded an MBE for her work. By then, she had already established herself as a doctor with a deep interest in public health and, in particular, the welfare of children.

She would go on to help found St Ultan's Hospital for Infants on Charlemont Street in Dublin in 1919 and, six years later, the

Dr Ella Webb. Picture courtesy of the Airfield Archive, OPW-Maynooth University Archive and Research Centre

Teach Ultáin, nurses and infants. Picture courtesy of the Royal College of Physicians in Ireland

Children's Sunshine Home in Stillorgan to help children debilitated by rickets.

By the time Ella Ovenden, as she was then, qualified from the Catholic University (now University College Dublin) in 1904, there were about 100 qualified female doctors in Ireland. But, as she wrote a few years later, opportunities for women in medicine were improving only if the female doctor could show she had not taken it up as a fad, but as a serious scientific or philanthropic undertaking.

A doctor also needed to have a true love of the work because that was the only thing that would help a medical practitioner through the drudgery, disappointment and heavy burden of responsibility that went with the job, she wrote in a guide to the professions open to educated women.

Her own commitment was not in doubt. She came first in her class in her final medical exams, the first woman to achieve that honour. She won a Royal University Travelling Medical Scholarship to Vienna and was awarded a doctorate in medicine in 1906.

The following year in Dublin, she married George Webb, a mathematician and philosopher. She used her married name but continued to work, highlighting in particular the need to improve women and children's health.

In 1907, she was one of the 12-member committee behind the Tuberculous Exhibition, which travelled all around the country to transmit public health facts on TB 'woman to woman' and 'mother to mother'.

She advocated breastfeeding, set up baby clubs, spoke about the need for good nourishment and warned mothers of the danger of infections, urging them to bring their children to hospital before they were at death's door.

In 1918, she was appointed as anaesthetist at the Adelaide hospital and ran children's clinics there where she saw, first hand, how poor diet and living conditions contributed to childhood rickets. When, in the early 1920s, it was shown that UV light could help, she was one of the first to use the treatment. She wanted to go further and help children recover by moving them to a well-lit facility away from the city's tenements.

The idea of the Children's Sunshine Home was born and, with considerable help from Letitia Overend, a fellow St John Ambulance Brigade stalwart who anonymously donated £5,000, the home opened in 1925.

A number of years later, Dr Webb wrote to her good friend Letitia at Airfield House in Dundrum to say the Home was "one of the very few things of permanent value that I have accomplished". That singular accomplishment continues to live on as LauraLynn Children's Hospice, which opened on the same site in 2011.

CF

Surgeon-in-Chief Dr Ella G.A. Webb. Picture courtesy of the Airfield Archive, OPW-Maynooth University Archive and Research Centre

Kathleen Clarke

(1878-1972)

Businesswoman, revolutionary, politician, woman's rights activist, humanitarian and first female Lord Mayor of Dublin

When Kathleen Clarke took office as the first female Lord Mayor of Dublin in July 1939, her first act was to remove all signs of British authority – the mayoral chain and a portrait of Queen Victoria – from the Mansion House. "The struggle for freedom has yet to be accomplished," she said, "that is first with me, and after that, woman's rights."

Her forthrightness was saluted by fellow political activist Hanna Sheehy-Skeffington (see entry on Hanna Sheehy-Skeffington) who welcomed her, four months later, as a guest of honour at a Women's Social and Progressive League meeting. "Mrs Kathleen Clarke represents a triumph of personality and courage," she said, going on to praise the new Lord Mayor for speaking out when politicians tried to "put women behind" in the new Constitution [of 1937].

If there was one thing Kathleen Clarke was not afraid to do, it was to speak her mind. Even as a young woman, she did so, refusing to join the family bakery on William Street in Limerick, opting instead to follow in her mother's footsteps and train as

Kathleen as a young woman

She knew about the Easter Rising of 1916, but Thomas Clarke insisted she would not play an active role. He had another task for her; he wanted her to help reorganise the movement, which she did. On the eve of their executions, she visited Tom and her younger brother, Edward Daly, in Kilmainham Gaol. The experience left her more determined to continue her own political activism.

In mourning c.1916

a seamstress. At 18, she set up her own dressmaking business and three years later, in 1901, she was managing a firm in the city.

By then, she had already met her future husband, republican leader Thomas Clarke, although she said she had been "keenly disappointed" by their first encounter. Clarke, 20 years her senior and newly released from jail, was emaciated and stooped and showed none of the heroic qualities that her uncle had attributed to him. As she came to know him, though, she changed her mind.

They were married in New York in July 1901. They ran an ice cream shop in Brooklyn and later a market garden at Long Island.

They returned to Ireland in 1907 and resumed life in business, opening and jointly running two tobacconists in Dublin. The couple had three sons, but Kathleen continued to work and was involved in the emerging Republican movement. She was a founding member of Cumann na mBan, becoming President of the Central Branch.

LUCKY CHILDREN—The Lord Mayor, Mrs. Tom Clarke, is here presenting the prizes awarded in connection with the Fry-Cadbury Scholarship Scheme at Parnell Square Technical Schools yesterday.
("Evening Mail" Photo (376G).

July 8 1939

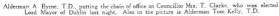

Alderman A Byrne, T.D., putting the chain of office on Councillor Mrs. T. Clarke, who was elected Lord Mayor of Dublin last night. Also in the picture is Alderman Tom Kelly, T.D.

Left to right:
Investiture as Lord Mayor, 1939
The Mansion House
Appearing on television in 1966

In May 1921, she was elected to the Second Dáil. When the Anglo-Irish Treaty was signed, Kathleen, together with the five other female deputies vehemently opposed it. She took the anti-Treaty side during the Civil War. Later, she became one of the founding members of the Fianna Fáil party. She was elected to the Senate in 1928 and to Dublin Corporation in 1930. She became the first female Lord Mayor of Dublin in 1939 and served two consecutive one-year terms.

As Lord Mayor, she helped found the Irish Red Cross – she chaired its first meeting in the Mansion House in 1939 – and took the lead in several projects aimed at improving the lives of women and children.

Kathleen resigned from Fianna Fáil in 1943, but continued to be involved in many aspects of public life. She moved to Liverpool to live with her son Emmet in 1965. When she died on 29 September 1972, she was given a State funeral and was buried in Deansgrange cemetery. Flags in Dublin flew at half-mast and thousands of Dubliners lined the streets to pay tribute to a woman who was outspoken until the end.

CF

'The struggle for freedom has yet to be accomplished, that is first with me, and after that, woman's rights'

Delia Larkin

(1878-1949)

Columnist, actress and trade union leader

Delia Larkin's words were still being quoted a century after she first wrote them. On the 100th anniversary of the Irish Women Workers' Union, the union she co-founded, one of today's union leaders recalled how Delia had said "all we ask for is just shorter hours, better pay than the scandalous limit now existing and conditions of labour befitting a human being".

Speaking in 2011, Ethel Buckley of SIPTU said Delia could reiterate that same statement today and not a word would seem out of place.

The need for continued progress does not, however, undermine the significant contribution that Delia Larkin made during her lifetime. Her brother Jim Larkin, the trade union leader, is never far from the public consciousness, not least because he is commemorated with an open-armed sculpture on O'Connell Street in Dublin, but his sister's story has been somewhat overshadowed.

Delia was born on 28 February 1878 in Liverpool. She was the youngest of the six children of Mary Ann and James

'[Female workers are] weary of being white slaves who pass their lives away toiling to fill the pockets of unscrupulous employers' – Delia Larkin

Delia Larkin. Picture courtesy of the National Library of Ireland

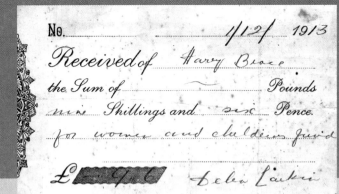

Receipt Issued by Delia Larkin for the Women and Children's Fund 1913. Dublin City Library and Archive

Liberty Hall as photographed by Keogh Brothers Ltd between 1910-1920. Picture courtesy of the National Library of Ireland

Larkin. The death of her father when she was nine years old and the family's subsequent descent into poverty forced her to abandon her studies.

In 1911, she moved in with Jim and his family in Dublin. Always interested in socialism, Delia embraced the Irish trade union movement.

She and Rosie Hackett (see entry on Rosie Hackett) established the Irish Women Workers' Union (IWWU) on 5 September 1911 under the auspices of the ITGWU, the union formed by Jim two years previously. The IWWU was the first women's trade union in Ireland.

Delia believed that female employees were "weary of being white slaves who pass their lives away toiling to fill the pockets of unscrupulous employers".

She also felt that a union could do more for its members than improve working conditions. To that end, she formed the union choir and a drama club.

A keen writer, she provided advice on topics from cooking to the Irish language revival in her column in the *Irish Worker*.

Delia represented the union's members within the suffrage movement and was an invited guest to Anna Haslam's (see entry on Anna Maria Haslam) celebrations at the election of Sarah Harrison (see entry on Sarah Cecelia Harrison), Dublin's first woman councillor, in February 1912.

Within a year, the IWWU had 1,000 members, mainly in Dublin but small branches were also established in Belfast, Cork, Dundalk and Wexford.

Delia Larkin, centre of front row, seated on the steps of Liberty Hall, headquarters of the labour movement, with members of the Irish Women Worker's Union. Picture courtesy of the National Library of Ireland

Delia played a critical role in the 1913 Lockout, which was sparked when employer William Martin Murphy banned his workers from being members of the ITGWU. The Lockout lasted from August 1913 to January 1914 and affected over 20,000 workers.

Jim was imprisoned in Mountjoy Jail for seditious language in October 1913, and Delia increasingly came to the fore, speaking at rallies and organising the feeding and clothing of union members and their families.

After the Lockout, Delia ran unsuccessfully as a Labour party candidate in the 1915 Poor Law elections. Increasingly isolated from the leadership of the Dublin trade union movement, she moved to London to work as a nurse.

When she returned to Dublin in August 1918, her application to rejoin the IWWU was refused, as was her application to join the Irish Clerical Workers' Union.

Over the next few years, she campaigned for the release of her brothers from prison; Jim was jailed in the US, while Peter was in Australia. She married Patrick Colgan, an executive member of the Workers' Union of Ireland (WUI), in 1921.

Still interested in drama, she ran a drama society for the WUI and also wrote for the *Irish Worker* in the 1930s.

Despite rumours of a rift between the siblings, Jim Larkin joined Delia and Patrick in their home in Ballsbridge for the last years of his life.

Delia died on 26 October 1949. Her latter years were marked by ill-health which, she said, caused "a very quiet life, quite against my inclination".

RW

Margaret Buckley

(1879-1962)

Trade union activist and first female president of Sinn Féin

For Margaret Buckley, the problem with Éamon de Valera's 1937 Constitution was clear; it treated "the women of the country as though they were half-wits".

His wish to banish women to the domestic sphere was not welcomed by other Irish feminists. Hanna Sheehy-Skeffington, Ireland's leading suffragette, led opposition to it, describing it as "a fascist model, in which women would be relegated to permanent inferiority".

De Valera's vision was the antithesis of Margaret's views. She was a passionate trade unionist and nationalist who believed in advancing the rights of women. She was arrested after the 1916 Rising and later interned in Mountjoy because of her vocal objections to the Anglo-Irish Treaty. She also worked as a Sinn Féin judge in the republican courts.

The year the Constitution was ratified Margaret became president of Sinn Féin, following in the footsteps of Cathal Ó Murchadha.

Margaret Buckley. Picture courtesy of Dublin City Library and Archive

57

She was born in July 1879 at Winter's Hill, Cork, the eldest daughter of Ellen and James Goulding. Her family were Parnellites and her own activism began when she joined the Cork Celtic Literary Society, founded by Terence MacSwiney.

A member of Maud Gonne's Inghinidhe na hÉireann, which later merged with Cumann na mBan, Margaret was in favour of the establishment of the Irish Industrial Development Society and was involved in protests against Edward VII's 1904 visit. She became president of the branch.

After she married civil servant Patrick Buckley in 1906, Margaret, who had worked as a teacher, moved to Glasnevin in Dublin. Her interest in the trade union movement developed and she took on the role of secretary of the Irish branch of the Women's Federation.

In keeping with her nationalist and feminist principles, she wanted the union to move on from its British origins and also to remain independent from traditional male-dominated Irish unions.

In the interests of achieving these twin aims, she embarked on talks with the Irish Women Workers' Union (IWWU) in 1919. Consequently, she became an IWWU official responsible for the semi-autonomous Domestic Workers' Union. In 1920, she opened its offices in North Great George's St and instituted a campaign for "good wages, fair conditions, to secure good service".

At this stage, she was already an active member of Sinn Féin, which she had joined after the Easter Rising. Secretary of the Michael O'Hanrahan Cumann in north Dublin, her Glasnevin home was often used as a safe house.

Top photo shows East Wing, Kilmainham Gaol with the Cumann na mBan corridor, 3rd floor below
Photos courtesy of Mícheál Ó Doibhilín

She was appointed a judge of the republican courts in 1920 and served alongside Kathleen Clarke, founder member of Cumann na mBan and Jennie Wyse Power, later a member of the first Seanad.

Two years later, Maud Gonne and Charlotte Despard established Women's Prisoners Defence League and Margaret became an active member.

She opposed the Anglo-Irish Treaty and served periods in Mountjoy Jail and Kilmainham Prison from January 1923 to October of that year. Later, these experiences would form the basis for her 1926 book *The Jangle of the Keys*.

During her imprisonment she was elected Officer Commanding (O/C) by her fellow prisoners. In her book, she recalled that during her time in Mountjoy, "in the case of hygiene, we agreed to wash out [our] own cells, but steadfastly refused to put a 'hand to' the corridors and staircases".

When the prison's deputy governor Patrick O'Keeffe told her to organise some of the prisoners to clean the general areas, she wrote that her response was emphatic. "'I can WHAT?' I roared. "How dare you suggest we become your charwomen!'" Eventually, several criminal prisoners were brought in to do the work.

When she was released from prison, Margaret returned to her work with Sinn Féin and the IWWU. Her 10-year-old nephew Séamus Ó Goilidhe came to live with her after his mother died in 1925.

The following year, Margaret represented Dublin at the Sinn Féin ard fheis in 1926 and in October 1934 she was elected one of the party's vice presidents.

She retired as party president in 1950, wrote a short history of her beloved Sinn Féin in 1956 and continued as a trade union official until the late 1950s.

Margaret died on 24 July 1962 at her Glasnevin home. She will always be remembered as the first female president of any political party in the State.

RW

THE
JANGLE OF THE KEYS

By
MARGARET BUCKLEY

WITH A PREFACE BY
MARY McSWINEY

DUBLIN
JAMES DUFFY & CO. LIMITED
1938

Margaret told the story of her incarceration in *The Jangle of the Keys*

Trinity College Dublin Archivist Ciara Daly with the original photograph of the first women graduates. Picture by Fennell Photography

The first women graduates of Trinity College Dublin were: *Back row, l-r:* Lizzie Burkitt Craig (modern literature), Eileen Frances McCutchan (ethics and logic), Muriel Lora Bennett [and sister of Louie Bennett, see entry] (modern literature), Bríghid Austin Stafford (modern literature). *Front row, l-r:* Anne Jane Sanderson (history and political science), Edith Marion O'Shaughnessy (modern literature), Eliza Beck Douglas (modern literature), Madeline Stuart Baker (Bachelor of Medicine). Picture courtesy of the Board of Trinity College, the University of Dublin. (Reference number IE TCD MUN Women 7/1)

milestones

The first women to graduate from Trinity College Dublin got their qualifications in 1906, two years after the college opened its doors to women. While those early women had new privileges, they still faced restrictions. There was a curfew, requiring women to be off college grounds by 6pm. When they were on campus, they had to wear a cap and gown unless accompanied by a chaperone.

Attitudes took time to change too. In the early years, women were sometimes considered 'a danger to the men', as explained in a book by the same name, edited by Susan M. Parkes. It was feared that a male student might unwittingly fall victim to a fortune hunter or be trapped in a bad marriage. Women, meanwhile, might find the experience of mixed education overwhelming. Early female students, however, performed disproportionally well in exams.

1906

The Women's National Health Association is formed to lead a crusade against tuberculosis and high infant mortality rates.

1907

The Irish Women's Franchise League (IWFL) is set up by Hanna and Francis Sheehy-Skeffington and Margaret Cousins. It pursues more militant strategies to secure the vote for women.

1908

The newspaper The Irish Citizen is founded by the Irish Women's Franchise League. Its motto is "For Men and Women Equally, The Rights of Citizenship; For Men and Women Equally, The Duties of Citizenship."

1912

Madeleine ffrench-Mullen

(1880-1944)

Labour activist, political nationalist, and healthcare campaigner

Madeleine ffrench-Mullen was involved in the Irish republican and labour movements, as well as campaigns for social reform. She joined the Irish Citizen Army in 1913, where she met Dr Kathleen Lynn with whom she founded St Ultan's paediatric hospital.

Born in 1880, Madeleine ffrench-Mullen was the daughter of St Laurence ffrench-Mullen, a surgeon in the Royal Navy. While it has been noted that Madeleine was born in Malta, the Central Statistics Office Ireland has since located her 1911 Census form which shows she was born in Scotland. Following her father's retirement from the Navy, the family moved to Ireland and settled in Dundrum.

St Laurence ffrench-Mullen supported the Home Rule movement, and local elections for the Irish Parliamentary Party were run from the family home.

Madeleine also had strong political convictions and was one of the first contributors to Bean na hÉireann, founded in 1908. The journal was the 'voice' of Inghinidhe na hÉireann, a radical

Madeleine Ffrench-Mullen.
Picture courtesy of ARTSTOR

Group celebrating Countess Markievicz's release from prison in 1919. Kathleen Lynn and Madeleine ffrench-Mullen are seated in the centre to the left of the Countess. Picture courtesy of the National Library of Ireland

nationalist women's organisation. Madeleine edited the children's column for *Bean na hÉireann*, and was drawn into the Irish labour movement to improve social conditions more broadly.

Although she lived in Brussels and Leipzig from 1909 to 1913, on her return to Dublin, she quickly resumed her political activities. During the 1913 Lockout, she worked in the soup kitchens in Liberty Hall – the headquarters of the labour movement and the Irish Citizen Army (ICA). She met Dr Kathleen Lynn (see entry on Dr Kathleen Lynn), who was a medical officer in the ICA, while learning first aid through the Citizen Army. She moved into Kathleen's home in Rathmines in 1915 and they lived together until her death in 1944.

Madeleine was a lieutenant in the Irish Citizen Army and in the 1916 Rising was stationed at the St Stephen's Green and the Royal College of Surgeons garrison. There, she tended the wounded, oversaw the commandeering of vehicles, and guarded the entryways to the Green. She was promoted to the rank of sergeant and, when the Rising failed, she was arrested and held in Richmond Barracks and Kilmainham Gaol.

Madeleine campaigned throughout her life to improve the living conditions of the poor. Having worked in the soup kitchens during the Lockout and with Belgian refugees of the Great War, Madeleine was acutely aware of the difficulties faced by the urban poor. Appalled by the high rates of infant mortality in Dublin, worsened by the outbreak of influenza and tuberculosis in 1919, she and Kathleen co-founded St Ultan's Hospital for Sick Infants, the first dedicated children's hospital in Ireland, at 37 Charlemont Street.

They began with just two cots and about £70. It soon became a highly successful and innovative organisation, aided by their ceaseless fundraising, and support from their wide network of activist friends and acquaintances such as Hanna Sheehy-Skeffington (see entry on Hanna Sheehy-Skeffington), Kathleen Clarke (see entry on Kathleen Clarke) and Maud Gonne MacBride.

Fundraising continued throughout the life of the hospital with Madeleine and Kathleen sometimes visiting the United States to raise money. These trips incorporated visits to paediatric facilities and they brought back pioneering medical advances to Ultan's. Madeleine worked tirelessly in the running of Ultan's and was secretary of the hospital until her death.

Madeleine was also politically active and joined Sinn Féin. She was elected to the 1920 Rathmines district council representing Harold's Cross. At the 1926 Sinn Féin Ard-Fheis, she argued for economic and social reforms, called for the party to support the implementation of State-sponsored school meals, and demanded an increase in the government's house-building programme.

In 1943, following the death of her brother Douglas, who had fought in the Easter Rising, Madeleine's health began to rapidly decline. In late 1943, she suffered an acute attack of cardiac asthma, and Dr Lynn temporarily placed her in a nursing home while she prepared for the Ultan's silver jubilee celebrations. Madeleine lived to see the 25th anniversary, but died shortly afterwards, on 26 May 1944. She is buried in Glasnevin cemetery.

MC

Letter from Madeleine to Robert Stopford thanking him for his donation to St Ultan's. Picture courtesy of the National Library of Ireland

Kathleen Lynn and Madeleine Ffrench-Mullen. Picture courtesy of ARTSTOR

Nellie Gifford

(1880-1971)

Republican activist and combatant, land and labour reforms campaigner, memory-keeper

Helen Ruth 'Nellie' Gifford Donnelly, more commonly known as Nellie Gifford, was a republican nationalist involved in many political and social reform movements. One of her greatest legacies was assembling a huge collection of Easter Rising and War of Independence historical artefacts.

Nellie was born on 9 November 1880 in Phibsborough, Co Dublin. She was the fifth child among six daughters and six sons of Frederick Gifford, a Dublin solicitor with offices at Bachelors Walk and Dawson Street. Nellie's mother, Isabella Burton, had been brought up in a family of 23 children. Isabella was a formidable character, staunchly Protestant, and a niece of the painter Frederick Burton. All the Gifford children were raised in the Church of Ireland.

Nellie's six brothers emigrated as young men and retained their parents' unionist politics, while she and her five sisters were all active in nationalist politics.

Nellie attended Alexandra College in Milltown and trained as a domestic economy instructor. After leaving school, she worked

This portrait of Helen Ruth 'Nellie' Gifford was taken when she was around 16 years old when her family lived in Rathmines at a series of six-month postings in rural areas across Meath for seven years. Here, she often stayed in labourers' cottages and observed first-hand the tough living conditions of the rural landless poor.

On returning home to Dublin, she educated her sisters on the land issue and was involved, in turn, with them in the women's suffrage movement, joining the militant Irish Women's Franchise League. A founding member of the Irish Citizen Army (ICA), Nellie gave lessons on camp cookery at headquarters in Liberty Hall.

DOMESTIC ECONOMICS,

OR ANOTHER IRISH STEW.

ENGLISH & SCOTCH LASSIES—"We've been instructed to teach you cooking."
MISS ERIN—"Thanks for coming. But you might have stayed at home, for up to the present others of your sort could make of things Irish nothing better than 'hash.'"

A cartoonist satirising the work of technical instructors like Nellie Gifford

A press photo of Larkin's arrest outside the Imperial Hotel. He is still wearing the beard that made up his disguise. Picture courtesy of the National Library of Ireland

'She forcefully campaigned for a permanent exhibition of modern Irish history. The material she collected now forms the core of the National Museum's Easter Week collection'

During the 1913 Lockout, Nellie escorted James Larkin to his check-in at the Imperial Hotel. Larkin was disguised as an elderly clergyman and, posing as his niece, Nellie did all the talking in case Larkin's Liverpudlian accent revealed his identity. From the hotel balcony, Larkin addressed a crowd gathered at Sackville Street (now O'Connell Street) triggering an unprovoked police baton charge.

During the Easter Rising, Nellie was stationed at the St Stephen's Green/ College of Surgeons garrison with fellow ICA members Countess Markievicz,

Madeleine ffrench-Mullen, Rosie Hackett and Margaret Skinnider. From the College of Surgeons, Nellie managed the garrison's commissariat. Faced with shortages, she organised the commandeering of foodstuffs from shops and bread vans. She also oversaw the cooking and delivery of rations to troops in her garrison and outlying posts.

Following the garrison's arrest, Nellie was detained in Kilmainham where, unbeknownst to her, her sister Grace married Joseph Plunkett.

After her release in June 1916, Nellie travelled to the United States to join a lecturing tour of fellow women veterans promoting Irish independence across the country. While in America, she married Joseph Donnelly, but the couple separated in 1921 and Gifford returned to Ireland with their daughter Maeve.

In the 1920s and 1930s, Gifford worked as a broadcaster and wrote pieces for the *Irish Press* and other newspapers.

Noticing the huge number of visitors to Dublin for the 1932 Eucharistic Congress, Nellie organised an exhibition of Easter Rising memorabilia for the National Museum of Ireland in Kildare Street. Calling on her extensive network of republican veterans, Nellie coordinated a sizable body of material representing nationalist organisations, the 1916 Rising, and the Irish War of Independence.

Following the huge popularity of the exhibition, she forcefully campaigned for a permanent exhibition of modern Irish history. The material she collected now forms the core of the National Museum's Easter Week collection.

Alongside the Easter Week collection, one of Gifford's most

The National Museum of Ireland on Kildare Street where the first Easter Rising Commemorative exhibition was mounted in 1932. Picture courtesy of the National Library of Ireland

important legacies was her preservation of the history of the independence movement. She was secretary of the Old IRA Association, and a member of the Old Dublin Society, an organisation founded in 1934 to promote the history of Dublin. Nellie was a founding member of the Kilmainham Gaol Restoration Society, and played an important role in the Easter Rising Jubilee activities in 1966.

She died in 1971, aged 90, at a nursing home in Rathmines.

MC

Helen Sophia Chenevix

(1886-1963)

Suffrage campaigner, trade unionist and social activist

Helen Sophia Chenevix was a prominent trade unionist, leading campaigner in the women's suffrage movement, and an energetic activist for social reform. She was born on 13 November 1886 in Blackrock, Co Dublin, to Henry Chenevix and Charlotte Ormsby. She attended Alexandra College in Milltown, and graduated from Trinity College Dublin in 1909 with a BA.

Helen was engaged in many labour and social issues, but it was as a suffragist that she came to prominence when, in 1911, she co-founded, with Louie Bennett (see entry on Louie Bennett) the Irish Women's Suffrage Federation. The Suffrage Federation was an apolitical, independent and non-militant umbrella organisation which sought to organise the increasingly diverse Irish suffrage movement.

It linked a variety of suffrage societies throughout the country and established connections with groups in Europe and the United States. Crucially, the Federation brought together moderate organisations such as the Irish Women's Suffrage and Local Government League, led by moderates such as

Helen Chenevix from the *Evening Herald*, 1963. Courtesy of the *Irish Independent*

Group from the Irish Women's Workers Union seated outside Liberty Hall (Delia Larkin in centre) protesting their ill-treatment in prison. Picture courtesy of the National Library of Ireland

Anna Haslam (see entry on Anna Maria Haslam), and the more militant groups such as the Irish Women's Franchise League, established by Hanna Sheehy-Skeffington (see entry on Hanna Sheehy-Skeffington) and Margaret Cousins.

It was also instrumental in the formation of the Dublin-based Irish Women's Reform League, of which Helen was made honorary secretary in 1915, and the Women's Suffrage Society based in Belfast.

During the passage of the Third Home Rule Bill in 1912, Helen was prominent in the (unsuccessful) campaign to include women's suffrage in the new Bill's provisions. Following the implementation of the 'Cat and Mouse Act' in 1913, she was among the Irish delegates invited by the National Union of Women's Suffrage Societies to take part in the Caxton Hall conference (a political meeting house in London).

The Prisoners (Temporary Discharge for Ill Health) Act 1913 – often referred to as the 'Cat and Mouse 'Act' – allowed authorities to release suffragists who had been weakened by hunger strikes from prison, but enabled their immediate re-arrest for minor infractions. Helen petitioned the Lord Lieutenant (John Hamilton-Gordon) on behalf of suffragists who had suffered under the Act's enforcement in Ireland.

Helen was also committed to wider social reforms. During the 1920s, she campaigned forcefully to raise the school-leaving age to 16 and maintained that families should be compensated by the State for any subsequent loss of earnings.

She was a member of the Bray and district trades council, and a councillor on Dublin Corporation where she served on the child-welfare committee and the National Maternity Hospital committee. In these posts, she worked for improved housing, State-sponsored school meals, and community playgrounds in the inner city.

Lá na mBan anti-conscription commemorative pledge. Image Courtesy of the National Library of Ireland

executive member of the Irish Trades Union Congress (ITUC) from 1946-56 holding the position of vice-president and president in 1949 and 1951, respectively.

In addition to her labour and social reform work, Helen was associated with the Irish Pacifist Movement and the Women's International League for Peace and Freedom. Following her retirement from public office she focused on working for nuclear disarmament. She died in 1963, and is buried in Deansgrange cemetery.

MC

She was also very active in the Irish Women Workers' Union (IWWU). She assisted Louie Bennett, her lifelong friend, to restructure the union along more professional lines. Together, they saw its membership rise dramatically from a few hundred in later 1916 to 5,300 by 1918.

She went on to become a leading executive in the IWWU, often heading negotiations between union members and employers. She was its general secretary from 1955-57. She was also an

A long wooden bench in the centre of St Stephen's Green, in the sensory garden, is dedicated to the lifelong social and political reform work of Louie Bennett and Helen Chenevix

Kathleen Behan

(1889-1984)

Folk singer, Cumann na mBan member, republican, socialist and 'mother of all the Behans'

When Kathleen Behan died in 1984, her friend of 50 years Matty O'Neill described her as the "noblest, proudest, and most vivacious of Ireland's daughters". Shortly before she died, she would still break into song, saying you're never too sick or too old for a song.

In her younger days, "she was a tall, spare woman with large expressive hands that moved in time with her songs", her daughter-in-law Beatrice Behan (Brendan's wife) wrote, recalling a woman with a beautiful singing voice and a repertoire of songs and ballads "the like of which she had never seen before".

Kathleen Behan said the world would never have known of her had it not been for her son, Brendan, but she earned fame in her own right as a regular guest on Irish and British television where she regaled audiences with her wit, repartee and unrivalled collection of songs. "I suppose what's kept me young has been good humour, singing and dancing, and jumping around in general," she said in her nineties.

Kathleen Behan. Picture courtesy of
Dublin City Library and Archive

Kathleen Behan, with Beatrice Behan. Picture from the Finnegan Collection, Dublin City Library and Archive

A portrait of Brendan Behan is being presented to Brunswick Street School by Lord Mayor Fergus O'Brien as Kathleen looks on with unidentified others. Picture by Billy Mooney, courtesy of Dublin City Library and Archive

Kathleen Kearney was born in 1889 into relative prosperity on Capel Street, Dublin. She was John and Kathleen Kearney's fifth child and her father owned a number of businesses on Lower Dorset Street. They fell into decline, however, and by the time her father died, in 1897, her mother had no means and had to send her three daughters to Goldenbridge Orphanage in Inchicore.

Kathleen recalled it as a dull, cold place and spoke of her "seven years of exile", but she said she got used to it and became an avid reader during her time there. Living in an enclosed space for so long turned her into "a nymph for fresh air", she said later, explaining her love of walking in the open air through Dublin city.

In 1916, she married Jack Furlong, a fellow republican. She was a member of Cumann na mBan and acted as a courier during the Easter Rising in 1916. All of her family were republicans she said (her brother, Peadar Kearney, wrote the national anthem) and she knew, and had great time for, revolutionary leader Michael Collins.

Shortly after the Rising, she went to work for Maud Gonne MacBride. "It wasn't a bad job, though Madame MacBride paid very little (my meals and that and a little money besides), but then I wasn't really a servant – more a receptionist," she recalled later in her autobiography *Mother of all the Behans*.

While working there, she came into contact with WB Yeats and many of Dublin's literary figures. She was the model for portrait artist Sarah Purser's The Sad Girl, which is now in the National Gallery of Ireland in Dublin.

In 1918, Kathleen's husband died of Spanish flu and she was left a widow with two small children. She got a job as a clerk with Dublin Corporation and married Stephen Behan in 1922, moving into a one-room tenement flat in Russell St.

The residents christened her 'Lady Behan' because she wouldn't join them on the steps to chat. "They were as common as ditchwater, but in the things that really mattered they were cream of the earth. We used to sing and dance every opportunity we got."

She missed that close-knit community when the family moved to Crumlin. She and Stephen had five children, a daughter and four sons, by then. Three of them, Brendan, Dominic and Brian, became writers.

In Crumlin, she earned a new nickname, the 'Red' because she took court action against over-charging shopkeepers who ignored price controls. "I don't support kings or queens, prime ministers or Taoiseachs. I have always supported the workers and will until I die."

She was true to her word.

CF

Kathleen was the model for *The Sad Girl* by artist Sarah Purser which is now in the National Gallery of Ireland in Dublin

Agnes A.V. Ryan

(1890-1971)

Businesswoman, founder of the Monument Creameries chain and patron of the Arts

Let us, for a moment, step inside Burton Hall, the luxurious 30-room Dublin home of Agnes A.V. Ryan, through the vivid lens of her granddaughter Barbara Fitzgibbon's memories.

Barbara lived there as a child in the early 1950s and recalls her grandmother, or 'the A.V.' as she was known, as a woman of amazing resilience. "Left a widow at 43 with eight young children, she built a thriving business – a chain of some 30 grocery shops in Dublin – and raised an independent and enterprising family."

Barbara continues: "Memories of my grandmother were of a very busy lady, whose chauffeur we suspected was also her bodyguard. She was extremely good to all her household staff at Burton Hall, and thoughtful of their needs. She maintained a magnificent home and wonderful kitchen garden, and I will never forget the smell of ripe peaches within one of the large glasshouses. She had a prizewinning herd of dairy cows, and essential bull, and was certainly way ahead of her time."

Agnes Veronica (A.V.) Ryan was one of 14 children born on 3 April 1890 in Solohead, Tipperary, to farmer Patrick Harding and

All pictures courtesy of
Agnes Ryan's family

Cover of Agnes's daughter Íde M Ní Riain's book 'The Life and Times of A.V. Ryan'

Agnes A.V. Ryan photographed by Charlie Godson of Rathmines

his wife Katie. In her mid-teens, determined not to pursue the path in teaching her mother had mapped out for her, she ran away to Glasgow, Scotland, and worked in her sister's grocery shop there. The experience she gained would shape her own career path as the entrepreneurial woman who founded Monument Creameries, a chain of grocer shops in Dublin.

The business grew from humble beginnings when she and her soon-to-be husband Seamus Ryan, a former creamery manager, leased a premises on Parnell Street in Dublin in 1918. The story goes that she looked out the window and saw the monument to her hero Charles Stewart Parnell and took it as a good omen. She named the nascent business Monument Creamery, the first word a nod to Parnell, the second, recognition of her husband's creamery background.

The shop, just off O'Connell Street, was an instant hit, drawing crowds of customers with its fresh farm produce: butter, cheese, bacon, milk and bread transported by train from farms in Tipperary. The following year, the couple married, despite objections from Agnes's mother, and after the ceremony at the Pro-Cathedral, situated conveniently near their shop, they went straight back to work.

The couple were ardent nationalists and, when a second shop opened in Camden Street in 1920, both premises were used as safe houses for the IRA. Ammunition was hidden in the bottom of butter boxes and transported around the city. Agnes, however, was deeply disillusioned by the bitterness of the Civil War in 1922 and lost all interest in politics. Her husband, by contrast, was deeply involved in the fledging Fianna Fáil party and went on to be a senator.

Staff outside a branch of the Monument Creamery

had lately courted her, and flattered her, now looked the other way when they met her in the street. Agnes replied by buying a new car, one of the first Daimlers to be seen in Dublin."

She went on to buy Burton Hall in 1938 and continued to oversee a thriving business that, at its peak, employed 500 people in 26 shops, a pub, two bakeries and two tearooms. Agnes was also an enthusiastic supporter of the Arts, buying works from Jack B Yeats, among others.

In 1966, Agnes A.V. Ryan finally sold Monument Creameries when supermarkets were in the ascendant. She died on 5 May 1971 and is buried beside her husband in Glasnevin cemetery in Dublin.

While the memory of her husband and some of her children, such as Hollywood actress Kathleen Ryan, has lived on, her great-granddaughter Dr Sarah Fitzgibbon says Agnes's role has been diminished. Now, it's her time.

CF

Meantime, business was booming. Then, the unthinkable happened. Just as the couple was considering further expansion, Agnes's husband died suddenly at the age of 40 in 1933. As he was close to the then Taoiseach Éamon de Valera, he was given a State funeral.

Agnes A.V. Ryan was left to run a business, raise her eight children – and face rumours, as her daughter Íde M. Ní Riain recounts in The life and times of Mrs A.V. Ryan (née Agnes Harding) of the Monument Creameries: "Only a fortnight after the Senator's death and impressive funeral a rumour rose, as if from nowhere, saying that he had died bankrupt. People who

The 30-room Burton Hall painted by Agnes Ryan's daughter Sr Íde. The house is now used as a centre for people with mental illness, run by St John of Gods. Picture courtesy of Agnes's family

DR. DOROTHY PRICE.
VISITING PHYSICIAN TO THIS HOSPITAL
FROM 1923 TILL HER DEATH IN 1954.
HER BEST MEMORIAL WILL EVER BE HER
PIONEER WORK IN PRIMARY TUBERCULOSIS
AND B.C.G.

Dorothy Stopford Price

(1890-1954)

Doctor and public health pioneer who introduced the tuberculosis (TB) vaccine to Ireland

Throughout her professional life, Dorothy Stopford Price worked to stop TB's deadly progress throughout the Irish population. She saw, first-hand, at St Ultan's Hospital, the toll the disease had taken.

Dorothy's father had died of typhoid fever in 1902 and perhaps this childhood loss inspired an interest in immunisation. That interest was later stoked when, as a medical student in Trinity College Dublin, she cared for victims of the Spanish Flu epidemic, both living and dead, conducting post-mortem examinations after her shifts at the Meath Hospital.

She was born in 1890, the third of four children. Her father Jemmett worked for the British-run civil service in Dublin, while her mother Constance was the daughter of Evory Kennedy, master of the Rotunda Lying-In (maternity) Hospital from 1833 to 1840.

Her family was steeped in the history of the Church of Ireland, yet she would become a Sinn Féin sympathiser after the momentous events of the 1916 Rising. Her aunt was Alice

Dorothy Stopford Price. Picture courtesy of the Royal College of Physicians in Ireland

 τeαc ulτάιn,
37 CHARLEMONT STREET,
DUBLIN.

Stopford Green (see entry on Alice Stopford Green), a historian and supporter of constitutional nationalism.

Dorothy spent the Easter holidays of 1916 at the Under-Secretary's Lodge in the Phoenix Park, now Áras an Uachtaráin. The seismic events of Easter Week had a profound impact on the young student. After her graduation in 1921, Dorothy moved to West Cork to work at the Kilbrittain Dispensary. She became medical officer to the local IRA brigade and gave first-aid lectures to the women's republication society, Cumann na mBan.

In 1925, Dorothy married district justice and historian Liam Price. The couple lived at Fitzwilliam Square in Dublin, while Dorothy worked in St Ultan's Hospital. The hospital, run by Dr Kathleen Lynn (see entry on Dr Kathleen Lynn) encouraged its doctors to be innovators. It supported Dorothy when she sought out new approaches to tackle TB.

Dorothy, who devoted her Master's thesis to childhood TB, lamented that "doctors in Ireland did not read or visit German-speaking centres and took everything via England". She learned German and researched how countries, including Germany, Austria and Sweden, were tackling the disease.

In 1931, during a visit to Vienna, she saw how Professor Franz Hamburger used an ointment to diagnose TB, and she wrote: "It is extraordinary that tuberculosis in children should have been a closed book to Ireland for 20 years after methods of diagnosis were well established on the continent, and at least ten years after methods of treatment had been evolved".

In Sweden, she witnessed clinical trials of the BCG, or Bacillus Calmette-Guérin, vaccine and she introduced it to St Ultan's in 1937.

Teach Ultáin Infants Hospital, Charlemont Street
Picture courtesy of the Royal College of
Physicians in Ireland

Not everyone in Irish society appreciated her innovation, as Anne MacLellan describes in her biography of Catholic Archbishop of Dublin John Charles McQuaid. He tried to halt her progress.

Dorothy wanted to set up an Irish Anti-Tuberculosis League, but McQuaid objected to the number of Protestant doctors in the proposed League and her vision never materialised.

She was, however, nominated for the World Health Organisation Leon Bernard prize for her contribution to social medicine and, in 1949, she was asked by then Health Minister Noel Browne to lead a committee to launch a BCG vaccination campaign throughout the country.

Dorothy died in 1954, but she left a crucial legacy with many thousands of lives saved through her groundbreaking work pioneering the use of the TB vaccination.

RW

Visit of the British Medical Association to Teach Ultáin in 1933. Picture courtesy of the Royal College of Physicians in Ireland

Máire (Molly) Gill

(1891-1977)

Political activist and president of the Camogie Association

Molly Gill received a medal for her involvement in the War of Independence and went on to be a staunch opponent of the Anglo-Irish Treaty during the Civil War. The future president of Ireland's Camogie Association spent six months in Kilmainham Gaol in 1923 after she was discovered with a notice for a meeting of the Irish Republican Prisoners Dependents' Fund and a copy of a Cumann na mBan magazine.

Undaunted by her experiences, she returned to her work as the main typesetter at Cuala Industries, the private printing press set up by Elizabeth and Lily Yeats, sisters of WB, which played a crucial role in the Celtic Revival of the early 20th century.

Molly was the longest-serving staff member at Cuala, outliving even the founders, and her work there had a profound influence on the young woman.

She was born on 24 March, 1891, one of four girls in a family of seven. Her older sister Jane worked for the arts and crafts cooperative, Dún Emer Industries, which was established by Elizabeth and Lily Yeats and Evelyn Gleeson.

Máire Molly Gill. Picture from the Loretta Clarke Murray Collection, courtesy of John J. Burns Library, Boston College

J. Rea, 64 Grafton St Dublin.
Ever Truly yours.
Máire Gill
1930.

Molly (front centre with cup) captained the Croke team to League and Championship honours in 1927

All pictures from the Loretta Clarke Murray Collection, courtesy of John J. Burns Library, Boston College

Molly was 17 when she went to work at Dún Emer after her sister got married. Shortly afterwards, Elizabeth and Lily Yeats left to set up Cuala which specialised in publishing Irish authors such as Lady Gregory, JM Synge and their brother WB Yeats. It was staffed solely by women, and Molly worked there until 1969.

Molly would later say: "The Yeats' mothered and fathered the girls [at Cuala], sent us to the Abbey and the opera. They arranged Irish classes for us."

She adopted the Irish spelling of her name, Máire Ní Ghiolla and moved in the same circle as WB Yeats and Maud Gonne, founder of the Irish nationalist women's organisation, Inghinidhe na hÉireann.

Molly joined Inghinidhe na hÉireann. In 1914, the group merged with the newly created Cumann na mBan, which aimed to operate as a female auxiliary to the Irish Volunteers.

Molly, one of the first members of Cumann na mBan, took up camogie and was a member of Croke's Football and Hurling Club, alongside Harry Boland. She became immersed in the organisation and was a founding member when the Dublin Board of Cumann Camógaíocht na nGael (the Camogie Association) was established in 1915.

She marched with the group at the funeral of Fenian leader Jeremiah O'Donovan Rossa and heard Padraig Pearse's graveside oration declaring "Ireland unfree shall never be at peace", widely seen as a call to arms that would result in the Easter Rising of 1916.

Molly was the longest-serving staff member at Cuala Press, set up by Elizabeth and Lily Yeats. Picture courtesy of the Board of Trinity College Dublin

Although Molly's role in the Rising is undocumented to date, it is known that she was a member of the executive committee of the Irish Republican Prisoners Dependents' Fund.

By 1922, she was one of Dublin's most prominent referees. The following year, she was elected as the first president (ardchomhairle) of Cumann Camógaíocht na nGael, camogie's ruling body, a role she filled for 18 years. She represented the sport on the organising committee of the Tailteann Games and captained Dublin to victory in the first All-Ireland final in 1932.

Molly died in 1977. Decades later, in 2016, a collection of her letters on sale at Adams Auctioneers were described as "a valuable illustration of the busy lives of those who were active supporters and foot-soldiers in the Republican movement".

RW

Action from a 1930s Camogie game
Picture from the Loretta Clarke Murray Collection, courtesy of John J. Burns Library, Boston College

'The Yeats [sisters] mothered and fathered the girls [at Cuala Press], sent us to the Abbey and the opera. They arranged Irish classes for us'

Rosie Hackett

(1893-1976)

Activist, trade union leader, printer and co-founder of the Irish Women Worker's Union

On 22 April 1916, Rosie Hackett was the first woman to lay eyes on the Proclamation of the Irish Republic when it was printed at Liberty Hall, headquarters of the Irish Citizen Army, on Eden Quay in Dublin.

"I was the first that was allowed in to the printing during the Proclamation being done. Madam herself [Countess Markievicz] was kicking up a row because she wasn't let in," Rosie, herself a trained printer, told broadcaster Donncha Ó Dúlaing in 1971.

During the Easter Rising, two days later, she was stationed in the first-aid station in the St Stephen's Green garrison, which was under heavy fire. "It was very exciting there," she said in a witness statement in 1951. "[Commandant Michael] Mallin was fired on, and the bullet went through his hat; and Madam [second in command, Countess Markievicz] was fired on, and it took a piece out of the heel of her boot."

After the Rising, she was arrested and jailed for ten days, but continued to work for independence when released. By then,

By 1911, Rosie was working at Jacob's Biscuits, a factory where working conditions were so poor that trade union leader Jim Larkin said they would send workers "from this earth 20 years before their time". When the male workers went on strike in August 1911, Rosie helped to galvanise support among the 3,000 women workers and win better pay and conditions.

Perhaps learning from this experience, two weeks later, Rosie Hackett and Delia Larkin (see entry on Delia Larkin) founded the Irish Women Workers' Union (IWWU) under the auspices of the Irish Transport and General Workers' Union (ITGWU). She had just turned 18.

In 2014, Dublin City Council named a bridge after Rosie Hackett, the first in the city to be named after a woman. Picture courtesy of Dublin City Council

She was active during the widespread industrial action of the 1913 Lockout when she again rallied women at Jacob's to go on strike in solidarity with the tram workers. Like tens of thousands of other Dublin workers, they were locked out of their workplaces by employers.

Rosie never returned to Jacob's, taking up work as a clerk with the IWWU at Liberty Hall where she also trained as a printer.

she also had several years of trade union activism behind her.

Rosanna 'Rosie' Hackett was born into poor circumstances in 1893, the first of barber John Hackett and his wife Rosanna's two daughters. Her father died when Rosie was eight and her mother worked as a housekeeper before marrying again in 1903. She and her second husband, Patrick Gray, a labourer, had three sons together.

On the first anniversary of the execution of the Easter Rising leaders, Rosie – with help from Helena Molony, Jinny Shanahan and Brigid Davis – went up on the roof of Liberty

Hall, barricaded the windows and doors, and erected a big poster that read: "James Connolly Murdered, May 12th, 1916."

Thousands of people gathered along the quays as some 400 policemen surrounded Liberty Hall. It took them an hour to get in. No one was arrested, because as Rosie commented later. "Of course, if it took four hundred policemen to take four women, what would the newspapers say?"

When, in 1918, the women's union broke away from the ITGWU, Rosie ran the women's section of ITGWU no. 1 branch as well as the union's shop on Eden Quay.

In 1970, that union presented her with a gold medal to recognise her long service. More than four decades later, in 2014, Dublin City Council voted to name a bridge over the River Liffey in her honour, the first bridge in the city to be named after a woman.

At the time, her nephew John Gray said she might find the honour strange, but it was a fitting tribute to "an extraordinary, ordinary woman".

CF

Female employees at Jacob's Biscuit Factory icing and decorating biscuits in 1898. Rosie later organised a strike at the factory to improve working conditions. Picture courtesy of Valeo Foods & Dublin City Library and Archive

'No one was arrested, because as Rosie commented later. "Of course, if it took four hundred policemen to take four women, what would the newspapers say?"'

Teresa Deevy

(1894-1963)

Playwright who gave a voice to women

David Clarke once offered this vivid image of his grand-aunt, playwright Teresa Deevy: *"I like to think of Tessa dashing out of her flat on Waterloo Road [Dublin] in the morning, rescuing the remains of her tall old bicycle from the bushes where she had thrown it the previous evening and rushing into Grafton Street to meet my grandfather — with a metal coat hanger still hanging from her coat."*

The flat on Waterloo Road, which she shared with her sister Nell, was at the hub of 1930s Dublin literary life. Fellow dramatist Lennox Robinson, artist Jack B Yeats, actress Ria Mooney and writer Frank O'Connor were all regular visitors.

Nell acted as Teresa's 'ears', as she went deaf after contracting Meniere's disease while studying at University College Dublin. She had hoped to follow a career in teaching but, instead, left for London in 1914 to learn to lip-read.

Over the next five years, she deepened her interest in theatre and resolved to be a dramatist. Her first plays were written under the pen-name D.V. Goode and while those early plays

Teresa Deevy was known for her modern plays highlighting the social constraints on women. Picture courtesy of Teresa's family

Teresa and her sister Nell (far left) with Frank Carney. Picture courtesy of Teresa's family

By 1925, she was submitting plays to the Abbey Theatre but it was 1930 before her first play Reapers was staged. Critic Abraham Jacob Leventhal described it as "epoch-making". Another five plays followed in as many years. When, in 1936, St. John Ervine saw her most famous play, Katie Roche, he wrote in The Observer: "Miss Deevy may be a genius."

When her play Temporal Powers jointly won the prize for new playwrights in 1932, Frank O'Connor wrote in a letter to her: "Nothing since the Playboy has excited me so much." Her work was praised as literary and original and it focused on women on the margins seeking a way out. However, it fell from favour in the deeply conservative Ireland of the late 1930s.

This prompted her to pursue a career writing plays for RTE and BBC radio and television. Her plays were produced in Waterford, Dublin, London and New York throughout the 1950s, but were largely forgotten after her death in 1963.

were never produced, she would go on to become known for her modern plays highlighting and challenging the social conventions that constrained women's lives.

Teresa Deevy was born into a devout Catholic family in Waterford in 1894, the youngest of Edward and Mary Deevy's 13 children. When she returned to her home city from London in 1919, she joined the local branch of Cumann na mBan and, despite family disapproval, visited republican prisoners in jail.

Another three decades passed before Judy Friel directed a production of *Katie Roche* in the Peacock in Dublin. In 2010, the very play that was turned down by the Abbey Theatre in the 1930s – *Wife to James Whelan* – was revived and produced on Broadway by Jonathan Bank of Mint Theater Company.

"An Irishwoman back from obscurity," said the *New York Times*.

Her papers, discovered in a green suitcase under a bed, are now in an archive in Maynooth University and her work and legacy were recalled by that institution and Waterford Institute of Technology (WIT) in a 2021 conference, the first ever dedicated to her.

At the time, Dr Úna Kealy, WIT lecturer in theatre studies, said: "A new generation of women trying to negotiate their way in the world have much to learn from Teresa Deevy."

CF

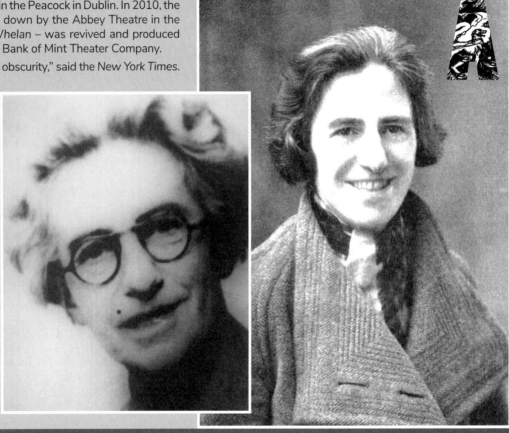

Portrait taken by Olaf Deevy

Teresa in 1938. Picture courtesy of the Abbey Theatre Archive

Evie Hone

(1894-1955)

Painter, stained-glass artist and pioneer of Cubism

Three years after her death, an exhibition in University College Dublin of Evie Hone's work, including drawings, paintings and stained glass, drew crowds of over 20,000 people. The artist had created stunning works throughout her career, including the renowned *My Four Green Fields*, a window that illustrates the four provinces of Ireland, and her depiction of *The Crucifixion* at the Chapel of Eton College in Windsor, England.

Evie was born in Clonskeagh, Co Dublin, on April 22, 1894, the youngest child of Joseph Hone and his wife Eva, who died just two days after her daughter's birth. Her family were artistic; according to the *Irish Times*, one of her ancestors was glazier Galyon Hone who was royal glazier to Henry VIII in the 1500s. She was also related to the artists, Nathaniel Hone and Nathaniel Hone the Younger.

Evie was 11 when she suffered from a bout of polio, which left her lame. She spent time in Switzerland for treatment, followed by visits to Italy and Spain. She moved to London in 1913 where she studied art, at times under the tutelage of Bernard Meninsky at the Central School of Arts and Crafts and

Evie working in her studio.
Photo courtesy of the *Irish Times*

The Cock, c.1948. Picture courtesy of the Hugh Lane Gallery

Abstract, 1925-1930. Picture courtesy of the Hugh Lane Gallery

Walter Sickert at Westminster Art School, where she met her friend Mainie Jellett (see entry on Mainie Jellett).

During a period living in France in the early 1920s, Evie and Mainie spent time with two advocates of Cubism – André Lhote and Albert Gleizes – who had a profound influence on their work.

But the Ireland of 1924 was not quite ready to appreciate that avant-garde art movement. A critic described paintings included in a joint exhibition held that year by Evie and Mainie as "no better and no worse than the productions of the average uninspired art student in her teens".

Evie, always devout, spent time with a community of Anglican nuns in Cornwall in 1925 but unsure of a vocation left after a year. She wrote in a letter to Mainie: "I feel quite at peace now about it and as certain as one can be of anything."

By the 1930s, Evie had tired of abstract art and her attention had been captured by stained glass. She studied in London with Wilhelmina Geddes, an important figure in the Irish Arts and Crafts movement. In 1933, she joined An Túr Gloine, a cooperative studio for stained glass artists.

Four years later, she converted from Anglicanism to Catholicism and was received into the Catholic Church at Blackrock College Chapel in Dublin by its president Dr John Charles McQuaid. He was an enthusiastic champion of her work when he became Archbishop of Dublin.

By that time, Evie's reputation had grown. My Four Green Fields, which was exhibited at the 1939 New York World Fair, won first prize for a work in stained glass. It is now in Government Buildings in Dublin.

Evie working in her studio. Photo courtesy of the Irish Times

She gained international acclaim with her work replacing the east window in the chapel of Eton College after it had been destroyed during the Blitz.

Evie, a founding member of the Irish Exhibition of Living Art, set up her own studio at Rathfarnham in Co Dublin in 1944. Almost a decade later, in 1953, she was elected an honorary member of the Royal Hibernian Academy. She died on 13 March the following year, but her legacy lives on.

RW

**The *Daily Sketch* record of the 1916 Surrender.
Photo courtesy of Mick O'Farrell**

**Sinéad Guckian's painting *Her Surrender*
now on display in Seanad Éireann.
Picture courtesy of Sinéad Guckian**

milestones

1916

Elizabeth O'Farrell, the nurse and Cumann na mBan member who stood beside Patrick Pearse as he surrendered after the Easter Rising of 1916, deliberately stepped out of the photograph. Later she said she regretted it when she saw how women and their contributions were overlooked in the new State.

Her feet were visible in the first photograph published by the *Daily Sketch*, but all trace of her was edited out in subsequent editions. Some say this was because editors thought the extra pair of feet (not necessarily recognisable as belonging to a woman) were confusing. In any event, the photo came to symbolise the 'airbrushing' of women and their involvement in all aspects of life from history.

On International Women's Day, 8 March 2021, artist Sinéad Guckian's painting 'Her Surrender' was unveiled in the Seanad. At the time, Senator Mark Daly said he hoped the painting "[rectified] in a very small way that historic wrong to Elizabeth O'Farrell".

1918

A limited number of women win the right to vote.

1918

'Lá na mBan' (Women's Day) on 9 June is a major success as women all over the country protest peacefully against conscription by British authorities in Ireland. Some 40,000 women signed an anti-conscription petition in Dublin alone, the *Freeman's Journal* reported.

1921

Frances Christian Kyle and Averil Deverell are the first women to be called to the bar in either Ireland or Great Britain, a milestone that makes headlines around the world.

1922

All women get the right to vote.

Josephine McNeill

(1895-1969)

An Irish diplomatic trailblazer, teacher, writer and art lover

Described as a rebel who became a servant of her people, Josephine McNeill was the first woman to head an Irish diplomatic mission. It was not, however, her first foray into politics.

As the wife of the Governor General of the Irish Free State, she was a renowned hostess in Dublin and London's political circles. But the Cork woman was also a teacher, a member of Cumann na mBan, an art lover, a musician and a writer, producing beauty

Josephine McNeill opens an exhibition of Irish paintings at the Stedelijk Museum in Amsterdam, with the city's Mayor Arnold Jan d'Ailly. Picture from the Elsevier Photo collection courtesy of Nationaal Archief / Anefo

> 'She did more than any three or four women usually achieve. And yet she left the impression of one whose full potential – perhaps from unconquerable shyness – was never fully realised' - Irish Times

columns for the *Sunday Independent* and the Irish language book Finnsgéalta ó India.

According to her obituary in the *Irish Times*, she "did more than any three or four women usually achieve. And yet she left the impression of one whose full potential – perhaps from unconquerable shyness – was never fully realised".

Josephine, daughter of James and Ellen Ahearne, was born in Fermoy on 31 March, 1895. A fluent Irish speaker, she studied French and German at University College Dublin.

She was engaged to Pierce McCann, commander of the Tipperary Brigade in the Easter Rising, but he died of influenza in Gloucester jail in March 1919 before they could marry.

A member of the executive committee of Cumann na mBan from 1921, Josephine said that although she carried guns for the male Volunteers, "at no time was [she] involved directly in any violent action".

In 1923, she married James McNeill, whose brother Eoin founded the Irish Volunteers. Josephine's marriage led her, reportedly reluctantly, into a diplomatic life where, one newspaper said, she gave the impression of a "very mannered woman of the world" who suppressed the rebel to produce the public servant.

James was then the Irish High Commissioner in London and he was appointed Governor General of the Irish Free State in 1928. However, the Fianna Fáil government of Éamon de Valera boycotted McNeill and he tendered his resignation in 1932, a few months early.

Both Josephine and James were unhappy with his treatment. Yet, when she herself was minister to Switzerland, Josephine spent time with Éamon de Valera when he was convalescing after an eye operation in that country.

After James's death in 1938, Josephine became honorary secretary of the council of the Friends of the National Collections, embraced Clann na Poblachta from its foundation in 1946, and chaired the executive committee of the Irish Countrywomen's Association (ICA) until 1950.

In 1949, she represented Ireland at the General Assembly of UNESCO at Paris and the following year, Seán MacBride, Minster for External Affairs, appointed her minister to the Netherlands in 1950. At the time, writer George Bernard Shaw described her as "a number one Diplomatist".

Queen Julianna of the Netherlands presented her with an Order of the Grand Cross when she left the country five years later. Further diplomatic postings followed in Sweden, Switzerland and Austria before Josephine retired in 1960.

In 1968, she was still prominent in public life and provoked a debate when she said Dublin was the dirtiest city she had ever seen. *The Irish Times* said it depended where she had been and at what time of day, but a columnist in the *Nationalist and Leinster Times* said her verdict carried considerable weight because it was based on her "travel and observation which was well beyond the average".

She died on 19 November, 1969. Her papers are held in the UCD Archives.

RW

An advert in the Evening Herald in October 1936 announcing Josephine's new weekly beauty column in the Sunday Independent

Dr Delia Moclair (Horne)

(1895-1971)

Mezzo-soprano, public health advocate, obstetrician and first woman assistant master of the National Maternity Hospital in Dublin

In 1922, Delia Moclair was unanimously elected the first female assistant master of the National Maternity Hospital in Dublin despite initial strong opposition from the hospital's more Conservative governors. Her three terms in that position earned her a place in the record books, but she also deserves inclusion for her pioneering work in obstetrics, public health and social activism.

She ran health and hygiene courses for young women, she pioneered pre-marriage courses, she highlighted the important role of midwives and warned that a culture of secrecy and shame was hiding the true extent of sexual violence against women and girls.

In 1930, she represented the Irish Women Doctors' Committee at the Carrigan Committee, set up by the government to review the Criminal Law Amendment acts and to consider the need for a law on juvenile prostitution. She and Dr Dorothy Stopford-Price (see entry on Dorothy Stopford-Price) told the committee they knew mothers as young as 13, and that many other young girls spoke of being raped only if they became pregnant.

Delia Moclair illustration by Holly Christine Callaghan

ST. MONICA'S BABIES' CLUB, DUBLIN.

Opened in St. Augustine Street, in June, by the Dublin Branch of the W.N.H.A.

Delia Moclair was involved in several new charities that supported mothers and babies. Credit. Picture courtesy of Dublin City Library and Archive

The doctors' call for sex and health education did not feature in the final findings; indeed, the Carrigan report itself was never published.

Delia Moclair was one of seven children born to Patrick and Margaret Moclair of Cashel, Co Tipperary. Her father was a noted member of the Land League and the family's eviction in 1888 was a high-profile case. They were not reinstated in their home until 1911 and, according to the *Freeman's Journal*,

Margaret Moclair never recovered from seeing her family "thrown out on the roadside". She died a few years later.

The eviction and the early loss of her mother marked Delia Moclair who, throughout her life, campaigned to improve public health and living conditions. Indeed, it was a singular achievement to get to third level, given her circumstances, let alone excel there.

She studied medicine at University College Dublin (UCD) and after her terms as assistant master at the National Maternity Hospital, she and Andrew Horne Jr, fellow assistant master, went to Vienna to complete postgraduate studies. The couple went on to marry and set up a private practice in Dublin.

Delia Moclair, however, continued to be very active in public life. She was president of the Women's National Health Association (and chair in 1959) and campaigned to improve children's health and eradicate TB. She was involved in several charities that supported mothers and babies and frequently spoke of the need to support young mothers.

She also supported new fathers, a fact noted in an *Irish Press* tribute which also praised her then unusual approach to early parenthood: "Her insistence that ... love and cuddling were as important to the new baby as feeding and changing, showed her wisdom and her knowledge of child psychology, since this advice was given when strict time-tables were in vogue for infant welfare."

Delia Moclair was also a fluent Irish speaker and an accomplished mezzo-soprano, winning several medals at the Feis Ceoil. In May 1922, the 'Notes by Jacques' column in the *Evening Herald* remarked that she had established her right to that year's gold medal: "She gave wistfulness to the words, 'I can nae get a wink o' sleep.' Others made it complaining or querulous."

She sang regularly at concerts and charity events raising money for a variety of causes from St Joseph's Orphanage on Mountjoy Street to Peamount Hospital, Dublin, where she was president of the board of management from 1963 to 1966.

As a devoted Catholic, she was a member of St Joan's Alliance, a Catholic feminist organisation that still works for women's equality in Church, State and society.

She had three children, a son Andrew (1931-46) and twin daughters, Margaret, a social worker, and Patricia who, like her mother, graduated from UCD with a degree in medicine. In the 1950s, Dr Patricia Horne worked as a surgeon in Africa before training as a psychiatrist.

In 2014, the twin sisters donated their father's wartime photographs to the Recovered Voices exhibition at Collins Barracks in Dublin. Dr Andrew Horne, attendant to the Royal Army Medical Corps, was one of the last officers to leave Gallipoli during the First World War.

Now, Dublin is honouring the 'recovered voice' of their mother too.

CF

The National Maternity Hospital. Picture courtesy of Dublin City Library and Archive

'She and Dr Dorothy Stopford-Price told the Carrigan Committee they knew mothers as young as 13, and that many other young girls spoke of being raped only if they became pregnant'

Brigid Lyons Thornton

(1896-1987)

Doctor, rebel and first female commissioned officer in the Irish Free State Army

Brigid Lyons Thornton was in her prison cell in Kilmainham Gaol when she heard the sound of shots fired to execute the leaders of the Easter Rising in 1916. She never forgot it.

A member of Cumann na mBan since she was a teenager, Brigid had been arrested for her part in the insurrection. She had helped to nurse the wounded at the Four Courts, the site of the fiercest fighting.

Released from prison in May 1916, she returned to her studies and nationalist activities in Galway and qualified as a doctor in 1922. That same year, she was commissioned by Michael Collins as an officer in the new Irish Army – the only female army officer commissioned until 1981.

Brigid was born in Roscommon in 1896, the eldest child of Patrick and Margaret Lyons. Theirs was a republican family. Her mother died during the birth of her third child and, at the age of eight, Brigid went to live with her uncle Frank McGuinness and his wife Kate.

Brigid Lyons Thornton. Picture courtesy of Military Archives Ireland

'The crowning tragedy came one night when I was called to see a new prisoner. Of all people, it was Mrs Tom Clarke. "We meet in strange places," she said. She was hurt to meet me there, and I was hurt to meet her. In every way, it was all too, too cruel'

Kilmainham Gaol. Picture courtesy of Michéal Ó Doibhlin

Brigid was a clever child, winning a prize for best Irish speaker in her school and receiving a scholarship to study medicine at University College Galway.

Her uncle was a staunch republican and the two travelled from Longford to Dublin when the news of the Rising reached them. During the War of Independence, she smuggled hand-grenades to the Longford brigade of the IRA led by Seán Mac Eoin. When Mac Eoin was captured, she carried messages from Michael Collins to him in prison.

She supported the Anglo-Irish Treaty and took on a heavy burden during the Civil War, acting as medical officer for female political prisoners, many of whom fought on the opposing side, in Kilmainham Gaol. "Many of those imprisoned there, I had known in the Anglo-Irish War, which makes it sadder still for me and often extremely embarrassing."

"But the crowning tragedy came one night when I was called to see a new prisoner. Of all people, it was Mrs Tom Clarke. 'We meet in strange places,' she said. She was hurt to meet me there, and I was hurt to meet her. In every way, it was all too, too cruel."

Later, Brigid met her husband, Captain Edward Thornton, in Nice, while convalescing from a recurrence of childhood tuberculosis. The couple married in 1925 and, after leaving the Army, Brigid devoted her medical expertise to paediatrics. In 1929, she was appointed assistant medical officer of health, and school medical officer for Dublin county borough. She played an important role in the BCG vaccination schemes that aimed to eradicate TB.

Brigid's interest in vaccination was lauded by President

Michael D Higgins in 2014, when he opened a housing development in Dublin named after her.

He said: "Brigid Lyons Thornton was a remarkable woman who is remembered both as a rebel and a doctor. After her implication in the Easter Rising and her release from prison, she continued to work for the welfare of the Irish citizens.

"Of all her achievements, the most remarkable is perhaps her fight against tuberculosis amongst the poor in Ireland, and her role in pioneering a BCG vaccination scheme in the 1950s."

Brigid, who volunteered at the Rotunda Hospital after she retired, died at the age of 91 in April 1987. She was buried in Toomore cemetery in Co Mayo, receiving Military Honours from the Western Command.

RW

Chelsea Fahy, Angela Mikailu, Fikewa and Fikunwa Popoola in 2014 at the opening of a new housing scheme, Thornton Heights, in Inchicore, Dublin, which was named after Dr Brigid Lyons Thornton. Picture courtesy of Conor McCabe

Dr Bridget Lyons Thornton's Emergency period certificate of service with ARP. Picture courtesy of Military Archives, Ireland

Mary Harriet 'Mainie' Jellett

(1897-1944)

The woman credited with bringing modern art to Ireland

In 1923, an exhibition of Mainie Jellett's paintings drew scathing criticism, with critic George 'AE' Russell describing her as "a late victim to Cubism in some subsection of this artistic malaria". He was not alone in his condemnation. The *Irish Times* published a picture of her painting 'Decoration' alongside an odd-looking onion under the headline, 'Two Freak Pictures'.

Yet, just four years later, that same newspaper would describe Mainie as "the only serious exponent in this country of the ultra-modernist school of painting". She went on to represent Ireland at the exhibition of art at the 1928 Amsterdam Olympics and, later, at the New York World Fair in 1939.

Mainie has since been hailed as the woman who brought modern art to Ireland. Curator of the 2018 EVA International, Ireland's biennial art festival, Inti Guerrero described her work as fascinating, "not only because of modernism but because you can see all the tensions and struggles that are linked to how to negotiate being modern and advanced and at the same time being highly Catholic and religious".

Mainie Jellett 'followed her own path despite opposition and misunderstanding' – art expert Máirín Allen

103

This religious theme ran through her work throughout her career, although Irish audiences did not initially appreciate it.

Mary Harriet Jellett was born on 29 April, 1897, the eldest of William, a barrister, and his musician wife Janet's four daughters. Theirs was an artistic family, and Mainie began painting watercolours at the age of 11. She studied at the Dublin Metropolitan School of Art under William Orpen and at the Westminster Art School in London, where she attended Walter Sickert's classes and met her great friend and colleague Evie Hone (see entry on Evie Hone).

Mainie won the Taylor Scholarship in 1920 and, with Evie, went to France the following year. There, they continued their studies under two influential Cubists, André Lhote and Albert Gleizes.

Her heart remained in Ireland, though, and Mainie returned in 1923. When she showed her work at an exhibition of the Society of Dublin Painters the same year, she was seemingly undaunted by the hostile reception. One journalist referred to her art as "sub-human", yet she persevered and continued to show her work at home and abroad in London, Paris, Versailles and Amsterdam. She was also writing, teaching and lecturing on modernism.

Her style evolved throughout her career and it has been described as a blend of cubism, religious art and Celtic design. She also designed a series of rugs featuring Cubist shapes and colours. She worked in set design for the Gate Theatre and Irish Ballet too.

In 1942, art expert Máirín Allen said Miss Jellett had some of the qualities of an ascetic and an idealist: "She has followed

'Meadow'. Picture courtesy of the Hugh Lane Gallery

her own path despite opposition and misunderstanding... her influence may be one of the most important in bringing our painters back into contact with European thought and European painting."

Mainie was one of the founders of the Irish Exhibition of Living Art (IELA) in 1943 along with Norah McGuinness, Evie Hone and Louis le Brocquy. Although she was its first chairperson, she couldn't attend the opening because she was seriously ill.

She died in 1944 and the IELA established a scholarship in her honour. In the decades since then, her standing has grown. She is now considered a central figure of cubism and abstraction in Ireland.

RW

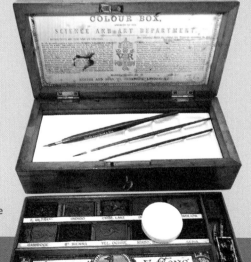

'Deposition', 1939.
Picture courtesy of the
Hugh Lane Gallery

(Mary) Maud Aiken

(1898-1978)

Violinist, musical school director, revolutionary, and key figure in music education and development in Ireland

When musician Maud Aiken died in a car crash on her way to formally open the Royal Irish Academy of Music's international summer school in 1978, the *Irish Press* noted that she died as she had lived – in the service of music.

"It was chiefly though her labours... that the Academy is in better shape today than ever before in its 130 years of existence," the organisation's vice-president John O'Donovan said at the time.

He thought she would be best-remembered as an administrator of the Academy where she had – as the "life and soul" of the Board and as chairperson for over 20 years – improved standards, finances and the reach of Ireland's oldest music school.

But there was much more to Maud Aiken, a woman whose revolutionary activity was only recently uncovered by her great-granddaughter, lecturer at Queen's University Belfast Síobhra Aiken, during research for her book, *Spiritual Wounds: Trauma, Testimony and the Irish Civil War*.

Maud Aiken lived and died in the service of music. All pictures reproduced by kind permission of UCD Archives

Maud and Frank Aiken cutting their wedding cake.
Picture reproduced by kind permission of UCD Archives

Maudie Davin, as she was in 1916, was well acquainted with many leading revolutionaries – including Arthur Griffith and Seán Mac Diarmada – who met almost daily at the Davin family hotel, The Ship, on Lower Abbey Street. Both Maudie and her sister Mina were known to use their musical activities as a cover for transporting messages. Síobhra dedicated her book to Maudie and three other women revolutionaries in her own family. The story of their activism had never been passed on from generation to generation.

Other family details, however, were remembered, as Síobhra recounts: "Maudie was a real socialite and fashionista; some of her tailored clothes and jewellery were passed on and I was lucky enough to be able to wear one of her Irene Gilbert opera coat and dress ensembles for my wedding. She spoke French, enjoyed entertaining visiting diplomats and corresponded with Jackie Kennedy and Grace Kelly."

She is described as "a wiry, strong little woman, a feminist who despite the height disparity when alongside her 6'2" husband, 'had the running' of him'" in *Frank Aiken: Nationalist*

and Internationalist, a book co-edited by Bryce Evans and Stephen Kelly. She met the man who would go on to be a Fianna Fáil minister and Tánaiste in playwright Máirín Cregan and Jim Ryan's home and later married him in 1934.

She gave up her job as director of the Municipal School of Music in Dublin as was usual under the marriage bar which obliged women to leave their jobs when they married.

By then, Maud Aiken was already an accomplished and respected musician. Born in 1898 in Dublin, the younger of John J. and Mary Davin's two daughters, she entered the Royal Irish Academy of Music aged 16. She excelled from the start, winning scholarships and medals.

When she was appointed director of the Municipal School of Music in Dublin in 1930, the School said her "record of distinctions" had made a great impression on them. It noted: "She spent four years at the Royal Academy and five at the London Academy of Music, where she was the leader of the orchestra under Sir Alexander McKenzie. She holds the highest distinctions in both Academies and carried off five gold medals at the Feis Ceoil and four at the London Academy."

It went on to note that she had been awarded the Beethoven Prize at the Feis Ceoil and had studied in Paris and Munich. She was also "full of tact with a great charm of manner".

During her four-year tenure, Maud Davin lived up to those high expectations and proved to be a dynamic director with noted organisational ability. She expanded the curriculum, promoted Irish music and introduced prizes and scholarships.

Sinéad de Valera and Maud Aiken after she was made a fellow at the Royal Irish Academy of Music in 1961. Picture reproduced by kind permission of UCD Archives

Despite the marriage bar, she remained a key figure in music education and development throughout her life. She was awarded a fellowship at the Royal Irish Music academy in 1961. She was involved in the Feis Ceoil Association (as vice-president and later president) and was also an early member of the 2RN, later Raidio Éireann, orchestra.

"She was amongst the most notable Irishwomen of her time," her colleagues at the Royal Irish Academy said in a tribute in 1978 after she died.

CF

Dr Thekla Beere

(1901-1991)

First woman to head an Irish government department

Thekla Beere was the eldest child of Lucie and Francis Beere. Her father was a vicar in Streete, Co Westmeath. She was a delicate child in her early years and chronic illness prevented her going to primary school. When she was 14, she had recovered sufficiently to take up a scholarship to Alexandra School, where she spent a year completing the primary curriculum.

From there, she moved into Alexandra College, where she sat junior and intermediate examinations. Her success in the senior examination enabled her to matriculate for the University of Dublin. She entered Trinity College (TCD) in April 1920, among the first generation of women to be educated there.

She transferred from English and German to the Law School, where she was the only woman in her class. She graduated in June 1923 with a first-class honours degree in legal and political science. She entered the labour market in the immediate aftermath of the Civil War – a time of widespread unemployment and political instability.

Dr Thekla Beere speaking at a reception in Iveagh House, to mark International Women's Day, 1984.
Photograph by Pat Langan, courtesy of *The Irish Times*

The President, Dr Hillery, with Dr Thekla Beere, vice-president of An Óige, at the opening of a photographic exhibition, "Fifty Years of Youth Hostelling", in the Bank of Ireland, lower Baggot Street, Dublin. Photograph by Jimmy McCormack, courtesy of *The Irish Times*

Despite her academic qualifications and many prizes, when she eventually got a job it was as a 'very lowly', as she once described it, temporary civil servant. Fortunately, her former professors at TCD recommended her for the Laura Spelman Rockefeller Memorial (LSRM) scholarship, which entitled her to two years' study and travel in North America.

There was a generous stipend, which enabled her to enrol in several postgraduate programmes, to travel widely in the United States and to afford an enjoyable social life. A number of job opportunities arose, but Thekla was determined to return to Ireland.

She was offered a position as executive officer in the Department of Industry and Commerce in recognition of her experience and skills. There was reluctance to promote her further because there were no women at higher levels. The marriage bar was an obvious obstacle to talented women such as Thekla.

During the Second World War – the 'Emergency' – the newly created Department of Supplies gave Thekla the opportunity to display her skills. Within six months of her appointment in 1943, she had been promoted to assistant principal officer and then acting principal officer, and she was closely involved with developments in transport, negotiations, financial arrangements and intricate legislation.

Thekla Beere with Mavis Arnold and Nuala Fennell in 1987. Photograph by Paddy Whelan, courtesy of *The Irish Times*

'While there was no doubt of her exceptional qualifications for the job, the fact that she was a woman reportedly created many concerns about protocols, at a time when male-only institutions and meetings were the norm'

She was appointed assistant secretary in November 1953, in acknowledgement of her unrivalled expertise on shipping, railways and labour issues.

In August 1959, Thekla Beere became secretary of the new Department of Transport and Power. While there was no doubt of her exceptional qualifications for the job, the fact that she was a woman reportedly created many concerns about protocols, at a time when male-only institutions and meetings were the norm. She left an impressive legacy of modernisation in the State-sponsored sector when she retired in June 1966.

In her retirement, Thekla chaired the Commission on the Status of Women which produced a groundbreaking report in 1973.

It led to the introduction of equal pay, in 1975; the removal of the marriage bar, firstly in the Civil Service and latterly across all employment; moves to end discrimination against widows, deserted wives, prisoners' wives and unmarried mothers in the social welfare regulations of the time. The Commission's recommendation on contraception, however, was considered to be ahead of its time.

Thekla led a full life in addition to her career accomplishments. She was a founding member and later President of An Óige, the youth-hostelling association; President of the Irish Film Society in the 1970s; she had a keen interest in the Arts, in theatre, opera and ballet. She died in February 1991.

MM

Prof Phyllis Clinch

(1901-1984)

Award-winning botanist who revolutionised the potato industry

The next time you enjoy potatoes with your dinner, take time to think fondly of Phyllis Clinch. She was the botanist whose scientific endeavours led directly to the rise of the virus-free version of this Irish staple.

During her career, Phyllis, an internationally recognised plant pathologist, became renowned for discovering complex viruses in the potato.

Thanks to her, this country became a by-word for disease-free potato crops and Irish farmers reaped the financial rewards.

Her brilliance was recognised by her peers. In 1943, she was awarded a DSc, or Doctor of Sciences, on the basis of her published work. Two decades later, in 1961, she became the first woman to win the Boyle Medal for Scientific Excellence.

Phyllis was born on 12 September 1901 in Dublin, the fourth daughter of James and Mary Clinch. She was educated at a Loreto school and attended third level at University College Dublin (UCD) from 1919. This was the start of a lifelong association with the university. She graduated top of her

Phyllis Clinch. Picture courtesy of the Royal Irish Academy

112

class four years later with a first-class honours degree in chemistry and botany.

She was awarded a post-graduate scholarship and was the first student supervised by Joseph Doyle, the newly appointed Professor of Botany. In 1924, Phyllis received an MSc degree after completing her thesis and received a research fellowship from Dublin County Council.

She then moved to London for a time to study plant physiology at Imperial College under the tutelage of Vernon Herbert Blackman. She focused on the biochemistry of conifers.

Phyllis was not yet 30 when was awarded a PhD in 1928. She and her supervisor Joseph Doyle had jointly published five research papers.

While her first post-doctoral position was as assistant to the Professor of Botany in Galway, she went to France before taking up the role. There, she studied cytology, the study of individual cells of the body, with Prof Alexandre Guilliermond.

After moving to Galway in the winter of 1928, she returned to Dublin the following year and was appointed a research assistant in the Department of Plant Pathology at UCD, then located at Albert Agricultural College in Glasnevin.

During the 1930s, the results of Phyllis's research revolutionised

the potato industry. She learned how to identify symptomless viruses and the ones that had a detrimental effect on potato stocks. She later focused her attention on tomatoes and sugar beet pathogens.

She was elected a member of the scientific committee of the Royal Dublin Society (RDS) in 1942. Phyllis became a lecturer in UCD's botany department in 1949. Some 12 years later, she succeeded her post-graduate supervisor Joseph Doyle to become professor. She retired in 1973.

The *Irish Times* noted that her tenure was "marked by an unprecedented and almost explosive growth in staff and student numbers, but especially by an impressive output of publications emanating from the department... She was always ready to recognise and encourage talent among her students."

Three years after she was appointed professor, Phyllis supervised the Botany Department's move from Merrion Street in Dublin city centre to UCD's Belfield campus.

She continued to be active after she retired. She was a member of the Board of Visitors to the National Museum of Ireland and was elected vice president of the RDS in 1977. She was also a keen bridge player and golfer.

Phyllis died on 19 October 1984 while on holiday in Tenerife. The benefits of her innovative research into plant viruses live on.

RW

A portrait of Phyllis Clinch by artist Vera Klute. Courtesy of Vera Klute, photograph by Eoin Kirwan

Mary O'Sullivan

Secretary to Dublin's Lord Mayors 1901-1942

Fanchea Gibson, manager of the Office of the Lord Mayor/Mansion House, recalls her predecessor Mary O'Sullivan

In 1901, Mary O'Sullivan started a 40-year career at the Mansion House as assistant secretary to Lord Mayor, Timothy Charles Harrington. Her name is not well-known or mentioned in the history books, but she was the trusted assistant of 13 Lord Mayors of Dublin, including Laurence O'Neill, Alfie Byrne and Kathleen Clarke. She also lived in and managed the Mansion House when Dublin Corporation was suspended between 1924 and 1930 and there was no Lord Mayor.

Her witness statement to the Bureau of Military History in 1951 gives a fascinating insight into her work and a personal glimpse into life at the Mansion House 100 years ago. As well as the normal secretarial duties carried out by past and current staff in the Lord Mayor's Office, her role also included personally representing the Lord Mayor in discussions with prominent public figures, such as John Dillon, leader of the Parliamentary Party, and the Lord Lieutenant and Chief Secretary James McMahon in Dublin Castle.

Fanchea Gibson, Manager of the office of the Lord Mayor/Mansion House

Éireann which met in the Mansion House. She refused entry to the Lord Mayor of Cork, Donal Ó Ceallacháin, as she didn't trust him. He gained access only when the Lord Mayor, Laurence O'Neill, looked out the window as Ó Ceallacháin walked away and called him back!

She was in charge of special correspondence delivered to the Mansion House for ministers and members of the Dáil and passing it on to trusted messengers. The danger involved in this is evident in her account of the time she hid letters at the back of a press just as the Black and Tans raided the Mansion House.

Having worked in the same role for the past 12 years, I find her account particularly fascinating. I can see similarities in our work, but also a vast difference in the personal risk taken in carrying out our duties. Her Mansion House was subject to raids by the British Army and was often surrounded by the military to prevent meetings being held there.

Mary attended meetings of the Anti-Conscription campaign in 1918, the first meeting of Dáil Éireann in the Round Room in

> 'She refused entry to the Lord Mayor of Cork, Donal Ó Ceallacháin, as she didn't trust him. He gained access only when the Lord Mayor, Laurence O'Neill looked out the window as he walked away and called him back!'

Groups of women and youths saying the rosary outside the Mansion House, Dawson St, Dublin, in 1921. Picture from the Hogan-Wilson Collection, courtesy of the National Library of Ireland

She was entrusted with the role of checking the credentials of people visiting the Mansion House, including scrutinising and verifying deputies coming to attend meetings of Dáil

January 1919 and she outlines the security at the Mansion House when the terms of the Truce were being agreed in July 1921.

Some 100 years later, I have worked with Lord Mayors on commemorative events marking these historic meetings.

Mary O'Sullivan describes the Mansion House of a century ago and tells us that the current staff offices were used as a Billiard Room, the venue for one of the Dáil Courts and the office of Minister for Local Government William T. Cosgrave.

My only regret on reading her statement is her obvious discretion. While this is a necessary, and admirable, part of her character, her personal views on the events she witnessed and people she met would have been worth reading.

The Mansion House, Dawson Street. Photo courtesy of Dublin City Library and Archive

I would have been particularly interested in her relationship with the first female Lord Mayor Kathleen Clarke (see entry on Kathleen Clarke) and her views on the growing restrictions on women's employment opportunities and the provisions on women's place in the 1937 Constitution.

Mary O'Sullivan is just one of the many unknown public officials whose work greatly contributed to the city of Dublin and the Irish State. But her unique role supporting the first citizen of Dublin during this very turbulent time in our history is one worth telling. I'm delighted she is being recognised and remembered in this book.

Mary Manning

(1905-1999)

Novelist, playwright and film critic

She received theatrical advice from Samuel Beckett, directed Jack Lemmon on stage and her children recall being serenaded at home by the Clancy Brothers. The last is not surprising, given that playwright, novelist and critic Mary Manning Howe Adams was so sociable that she even hosted a party in her retirement home a fortnight before she died.

According to Micheál MacLiammóir, who appeared in her first play, *Youth's the season...?*, "her brain, nimble and observant as it was, could not yet keep pace with a tongue so caustic that even her native city was a little in awe of her".

That debut, which garnered appreciative reviews, boasted a Beckettian touch. Mary had included a silent character named Egosmith at the suggestion of her good friend Samuel.

Later, when she considered selling some correspondence between herself and Beckett, he wrote to her saying there was "no question of your ever losing my friendship. I think of you often and with all my heart wish for you better days".

Mary was born in Dublin on 30 June 1905, the eldest of Fitzmaurice and Susan Manning's three children. Her father, a civil servant in the colonial service, died in 1918 while serving in West Africa.

Mary was educated at Morehampton House School and Alexandra College before studying acting under the tutelage of actress Sara Allgood and Ria Mooney, the first female producer at the Abbey Theatre.

Although information is scant, Mary appears to have played a significant role in Ireland's second wave of silent film production, which took place between 1930 and 1935. She worked first as a film critic, one who preferred European fare to Hollywood, then later as a filmmaker. She also co-founded the Dublin Film Society in 1930.

When she was publicity manager at the Gate Theatre, Mary founded and edited Motley, the influential magazine that included Austin Clarke, Frank O'Connor and Mainie Jellett among its contributors. Mary characterised the early 1930s as a period of "intellectual creativity which I've never known again".

In 1935, she emigrated to America where she married Harvard law professor and civil rights activist Mark de Wolfe Howe. The couple, who had three children together, set up home in Cambridge, Massachusetts. Two of her daughters, Susan and Fanny, are acclaimed poets.

Mary studied under the tutelage of Ria Mooney, first female producer at the Abbey Theatre. Picture courtesy of Dublin City Library and Archive

Mary wrote three novels, the first of which Mount Venus was published in 1938, and she continued her theatrical interests while living in Cambridge. Her participation in the Radcliffe College drama programme led to her directing Jack Lemmon when he played Christy in a student production of The Playboy of the Western World.

She was one of the co-founders in 1950 of the Poets' Theatre, a small theatre company in Cambridge that encouraged young poets and dramatists. Two years later, she convinced Dylan Thomas to travel for his first American reading. Later, actress Siobhan McKenna and playwright Brendan Behan appeared at the Poets' Theatre and, in 1955, Mary staged a production of Finnegans Wake.

After her husband Mark died in 1968, Mary returned to Dublin, working as a drama critic for Hibernia and the Irish Times. During this period, she revived her playwriting career, producing a critically acclaimed adaption of Frank O'Connor's novel The Saint and Mary Kate, which was performed at the Abbey in 1968.

She also penned a set of satirical short stories called The Last Chronicles of Ballyfungus, which were published in 1978. Two years later, she returned to the US and married Faneuil Adams, a lawyer based in Boston.

Mary was 93 when she died at Mount Auburn Hospital in Cambridge, Massachusetts, on 27 June 1999. "Boston will be a quieter, duller town now that it has lost the indomitable presence of Mary Manning Howe Adams, known to all as Molly," noted the obituary in the Irish Times.

RW

Peggy Dell
(Margaret Tisdall)

(1906-1979)

Singer, accomplished pianist and first female bandleader

At age three, Margaret 'Peggy' Tisdall was already learning to play the piano. At nine-and-a-half, she made her stage debut at the Empire Palace (now the Olympia Theatre) in Dublin while her father watched from the orchestra pit below. At 13, she got her first job at Woolworth's on Grafton Street, Dublin, playing piano to promote sheet music.

Although her father William, a musician, hoped the only child born to him and his wife Margaret Tisdall in 1906 would become a concert pianist, it didn't quite play out that way.

Before she reached 20, Margaret Tisdall had formed a band, the first woman in Ireland to do so. When the trio arrived to play in Rathfarnham, Dublin, the woman who booked the function looked at the band members – Peggy had her hair in two plaits, one of the boy-men was wearing short pants and another a skull cap – and said: "I wanted a band. I don't want three children."

When she heard them play, however, she changed her mind. Margaret Tisdall had embarked on a career that would bring her all over the world and win her international acclaim as a pianist, showband leader and entertainer.

She performed in all of Dublin's popular entertainment venues, from the Capitol, off O'Connell Street, to the Theatre Royal on Hawkins Street, before going to England in the 1930s. She was at the forefront of modern media there, appearing on the BBC with Jack Hylton when television was still in its infancy.

When bandleader Roy Fox asked her to audition, she became his first female

Peggy with Noel Purcell and famous English comic Tommy Trinder outside the stage door of the Royal Theatre in the late 1930s

vocalist and they played popular venues in London. They went to Paris to broadcast on French radio.

The pace was relentless. Peggy Dell – she adopted the stage name around then – recalled there were weeks when she performed four times a day at two different theatres. But she said she wouldn't have it any other way.

The bookings kept coming. She toured America with Jack Hylton and when the Second World War broke out, she returned to Dublin and signed up to play at the Metropole Hotel in the city. After the war, or the 'Emergency' as it was called in Ireland, she formed a six-piece band and travelled to dances and carnivals all over Ireland.

"I was a divil for punishment," she said.

In 1970, she was seriously injured in a taxi accident in Dublin and thought she might never work again. But her luck changed when Gay Byrne invited her on *The Late Late Show* to celebrate actor Noel Purcell's 70th birthday in 1973. She was such a hit that RTE, the national broadcaster, gave her a programme of her own, *Peg o' my heart*.

The following year, she won a Jacob's TV

Top: Noel Purcell and Peggy on stage at the Theatre Royal in Dublin. Pictures courtesy of Conor Doyle and Patrick Purcell

award. She was back in showbusiness with a bang. In her late-60s, she travelled to Las Vegas with the Variety Club of Ireland and told the Irish Times that she had stayed up all night playing the slot machines with Noel Purcell.

Looking back on her career in 1975, she said she had no regrets: "I'd do it all again exactly the same, if I had the chance, starting at the age of nine."

A final note: Peggy was an only child and had no family, so her grave in Glasnevin cemetery was unmarked. When Dubliner and music lover Rob Twamley heard that, he started a fund-raising campaign to honour one of Dublin's best-loved entertainers. A new headstone was erected on her grave in April 2022.

CF

Dublin's Great
Peggy Dell
Pianist - Variety Artist - Singer
Margaret Tisdall
1906 - 1979

Her Mother
Margaret Tisdall
1880 - 1954
Her Father
William Tisdall
1875 - 1926

*The Song is Ended
But the Melody lives on....*

Peggy and Noel Purcell. She told the *Irish Times* that she and Noel had stayed up all night to play the slot machines when they went to Las Vegas with the Variety Club of Ireland. She was in her late 60s at the time.

Picture courtesy of Conor Doyle who is campaigning to have the new pedestrian street on the Hawkins Street site called 'Theatre Royal Way'

Picture of gravestone courtesy of Rob Twamley

IRISH WOMEN WORKERS' UNION
1911-1984

... ALL WE ASK FOR IS JUST SHORTER HOURS, BETTER PAY THAN THE SCANDALOUS LIMIT NOW EXISTING AND CONDITIONS OF LABOUR BEFITTING A HUMAN BEING

- IWWU FOUNDER MEMBER DELIA LARKIN

AT ITS PEAK THE IWWU ORGANISED ABOUT 70,000 WOMEN, INCLUDING BOOKBINDERS, CONTRACT CLEANERS, LAUNDRY, PRINT AND ELECTRONIC WORKERS.

Outside the laundry we put up a fight
For a fortnight's holiday
They said we'd have to strike
So we keep marching up and down,
As we nearly did for half a crown
We are a fighting people
Who cannot be kept down

IN 1945, WOMEN LAUNDRY WORKERS SANG THIS SONG ON THE PICKET LINES AFTER THEY WENT ON STRIKE TO WIN TWO WEEKS ANNUAL PAID HOLIDAYS. NO ORGANISED MALE WORKERS HAD PREVIOUSLY DEMANDED THIS. THE WOMEN WON THAT RIGHT FOR ALL WORKERS.

IWWU Commemorative Committee, March 8, 2013

A plaque on Liberty Hall in Dublin commemorating the Irish Women Workers' Union and the laundry strike of 1945. Picture courtesy of Noreen Maher.

milestones

Female national school-teachers have to resign on marriage. In 1935, the Employment Act extends the marriage bar to include all women civil servants.	**1933**
The importation and sale of contraceptives is made illegal.	**1935**
The Women's Social and Progressive League is formed to object to proposed articles in the 1937 Constitution considered likely to diminish the status of women.	**1937**
Divorce is banned. In the same year, despite protests, the new Constitution states that the State shall "endeavour to ensure that mothers shall not be obliged by economic necessity to engage in labour to the neglect of their duties in the home".	**1937**
Bridget Mary Rice, the only woman deputy in the 10th Dáil, is elected in Monaghan.	**1938**
Kathleen Clarke is elected Lord Mayor of Dublin, the first woman to hold the office or any mayoralty in Ireland. *(See entry on Kathleen Clarke).*	**1939**
The Children's Allowance payment is introduced.	**1944**
The Irish Women Workers' Union organise a 14-week strike by 1,500 laundry workers.	**1945**

In a statement, the union outline conditions in its bid to secure more time off: "Laundry work is performed standing in a heated atmosphere causing, in hot weather especially, great fatigue, excessive perspiration and blistered feet... laundresses often worked from 8 a.m. to 9 p.m. in order to meet demand."

The words to a song were also printed and sold to raise funds for the strikers. The lyrics of the song are reproduced on the image of the plaque opposite.

The union won, securing two weeks' paid holidays not just for laundry workers, but for all workers.

Kathleen O'Rourke

(1906-1980)

Co-founder of the Central Remedial Clinic, physiotherapist, remedial gymnast and one of Ireland's first fitness instructors

In 1951, Kathleen O'Rourke, a remedial gymnast with a special interest in rehabilitation therapy, set up what would become the Central Remedial Clinic (CRC) in her Upper Pembroke Street flat in Dublin. Children were carried up three flights of stairs and treated on a dining-room table that was covered with blankets to bring them to the right height.

Both she and Lady Valerie Goulding were responding to the urgent need to provide aftercare for those left with disabilities after the polio epidemics of 1948 and 1950. With the help of orthopaedic surgeon Dr Boyd Dunlop, they established a clinic in Goatstown, Dublin, in 1954, before moving into a purpose-built centre in Clontarf in 1961.

Lady Goulding, an English aristocrat, was even persuaded by Kathleen O'Rourke to study physiotherapy, but later realised that her strength lay in using her high-profile contacts – from Princess Grace of Monaco, Louis Armstrong and Bing Crosby – to raise money for the centre.

The British League of Health and Beauty logo featured a member leaping through the air, but that was considered too risqué in Ireland. Bishop, later Archbishop, John Charles McQuaid insisted it be toned down.

Meanwhile, Kathleen O'Rourke, a native of Ballyconnell, Cavan, used her qualifications to work at the CRC. By then, she had a first-class diploma from the Liverpool College of Physical Education, a qualification as a remedial gymnast from Pinderfields General Hospital, Yorkshire and she was a member of the Chartered Society of Physiotherapists.

She also had several decades' experience with the Women's League of Health and Beauty. She trained with Dublin-born Mary Bagot-Stack, who founded the League in London in 1930. It was the first mass keep-fit system developed by women for women. Kathleen opened the first branch in Dublin in 1934. Within a year, more than 1,000 women had signed up to take the League's graceful but challenging exercise classes, set to music.

It was not all smooth progress, however. Kathleen's cousin, Bishop John Charles McQuaid – later Archbishop in 1940 – insisted that members wear skirts over immodest shorts, change the logo and remove the word 'Beauty' from the title, as it was too racy.

Nothing, however, dimmed the League of Health in Ireland's popularity. Kathleen O'Rourke won a wider audience with her weekly Irish Press health column in the mid-40s, the first one written by a woman directly connected to a physical movement organisation. She also gave several talks.

"To keep physically fit was a matter of vital importance to the individual and to the nation," she told members of the Rotary Club in 1940. Her words had influence. A number of hospitals – Cork Street Fever Hospital, the Meath, Dr Steevens and Peamount Sanatorium – and private firms such as Jacob's Biscuits arranged exercise classes for their staff.

The Irish League also attracted international attention. In 1949, in recognition of its work, Irish members were invited to take part in Lingiad, a universal sport exhibition in Stockholm,

Sweden. It was a singular honour, yet the Government refused to provide funding. Journalist Anne Kelly was outraged, writing in the *Irish Press* in June 1949 that the Irish gymnasts were "all dressed up in twinkling green and white uniforms, ready and waiting to go".

Childcare was an issue too. One of the 24-member team Isolde McCullagh, a fitness tutor herself, said she would have to bring her eight-week-old son to Sweden with her. In the end, she did just that and the League managed to raise enough money to finance a trip that was celebrated in the press.

Kathleen went on to establish the Dublin College of Physical Education (now Thomond College in Limerick) and was the first to set up antenatal classes in Dublin. She included men in the classes too, making them do their breathing exercises beside the women.

Her legacy lives on not only in the Central Remedial Clinic, one of the country's largest organisations dedicated to people with physical disabilities, but also at Fitness League Ireland which is still running more than 60 weekly sessions today.

CF

Kathleen O'Rourke led 24 Irish athletes at Lingiad, a universal sport exhibition in Stockholm, Sweden. The members of the Irish League of Health in Ireland had been invited in recognition of their work in Ireland.

Nora Herlihy

(1910-1988)

Guiding force behind the Irish credit union movement

By the time Nora Herlihy died, the credit union movement that she had started in Ireland 30 years earlier had almost one million members in 500 branches throughout the country.

She had trained as a schoolteacher and the experience of working with poverty-stricken families in 1950s Dublin had a profound impact on her.

According to Uel Adair, president of the Irish League of Credit Unions, "Nora recognised the root of the problem as lying in the scarce availability and poor management of money and resolved to identify a system that would allow people to gain more control over their finances."

Nora was born in 1910 in Ballydesmond on the Cork-Kerry border. She was the third of Denis and Nora Herlihy's 12 children. Her father was a teacher, and she followed in his footsteps. Although religious, Nora realised that she did not have a vocation after spending 10 months at a missionary congregation in Cavan in 1941. Instead, she devoted her considerable energy to helping the financially disadvantaged.

Nora Herlihy. Picture courtesy of the Irish League of Credit Unions

Broadcaster Marian Finucane at a wreath-laying ceremony in memory of her aunt in 2000. Picture courtesy of John Reidy

Tomás Ó Hogáin, a social economics student, and Seamus Mac Eoin, a civil servant, also shared her conviction and they asked Nora to chair a meeting on 9 December 1953 dedicated to the principles of the co-operative moment.

The following year, she and Tomás founded the Dublin Central Co-operative Society. A forerunner of the National Co-operative Council, it aimed to reduce unemployment and emigration.

Nora encouraged a group of her neighbours in Phibsborough in Dublin, including sisters Eileen and Angela Byrne (Aingil Ni Bhroin), to establish the country's first credit union in Donore Avenue in April 1958. In its first week, it collected a total of Ir£7.

By 1960, credit unions had been set up throughout the country, and the Credit Union League of Ireland, which was run from Nora's home, acted as an umbrella body. Thanks to Nora, who had developed contacts, it was affiliated with the Credit Union National Association (CUNA) in America.

She initially acted as secretary of the Credit Union League and then as its managing director. In both positions, she was an unpaid volunteer while also working full-time in St Joseph's girls' national school and travelling to the US and Canada on credit union research.

Nora was a key player behind the 1966 Credit Union Act and was pictured alongside President Éamon de Valera as he signed it into law.

In 1963, she was recognised by the board of the Credit Union League of Ireland as having made the greatest individual contribution to this country's credit union movement. However, just three years later, she was voted out of her role as managing director.

In January 1965, she was appointed principal of St Joseph's and she held that position until she retired in 1974. She died on

7 February 1988 on the 28th anniversary of the founding of the Irish League of Credit Unions.

In 2000, her niece, the well-known broadcaster Marian Finucane, who described her aunt as a very determined woman, attended the opening of a museum at the Ballydesmond Credit Union building dedicated to Nora.

The guest of honour was Nobel Prize winner and credit union leader John Hume, who said that Nora would be remembered as the greatest woman in the history of Ireland to date.

RW

Miniature replicas of Nora's bust were presented by John Hume, Nobel Prize winner and credit union leader, to her sisters, Sheila O'Carroll, Margaret Murphy and Sr Dorothy, on his right. Picture courtesy of John Reidy

'Nora recognised the root of the problem as lying in the scarce availability and poor management of money and resolved to identify a system that would allow people to gain more control over their finances'

John Hume with artist Paula O'Sullivan at the unveiling of her bust of Nora in Ballydesmond on the Cork/Kerry border. Picture courtesy of John Reidy

Hilda Tweedy

(1911-2005)

Women's activist and consumer champion

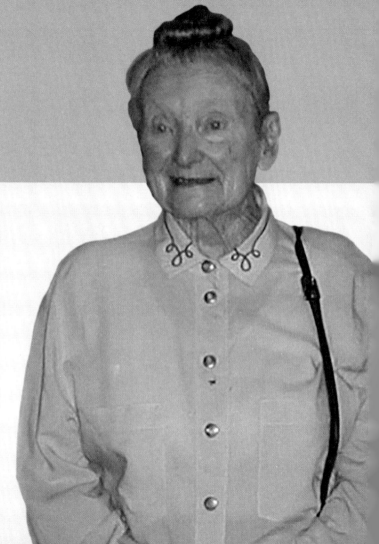

In 1952, the *Roscommon Herald* claimed that the Irish Housewives Association was "a medium of communication for Marxists" and that it had caused riots on O'Connell Street in Dublin. The remark was later withdrawn and damages awarded, but the charge illustrated the power that lay behind the organisation founded by Hilda Tweedy.

An instigator of what became known as the 'Housewives Petition', which aimed to alleviate hardship during the Second World War, and co-founder of the progressive Irish Housewives Association (IHA), she exerted a gentle pressure that Ireland's elite learned not to underestimate.

Later, Nuala Ryan, a former colleague on the Council for the Status of Women, said Hilda Tweedy had an unwavering commitment to radically improve the status of Irish women. She also did far-sighted work to protect the rights of consumers.

Hilda was born on 26 August 1911, the eldest of James and Muriel Frances Anderson's three daughters. She showed an interest in volunteer work from a young age; she was a member

Hilda Tweedy. Picture courtesy of Alan Hayes

An Irish Housewives Association protest from the 1940s
Picture courtesy of Alan Hayes

Hilda (centre) at a meeting of the Employment Equality Agency, 1978.
Picture courtesy of Derek Speirs

of the Girl Guides and the Children's League of Pity charity.

She went to Alexandra College and, in 1929, moved to Egypt where her father was working as a chaplain. There, she started a small school and began studying mathematics, as an external student, at the University of London. She returned to Dublin after marrying Robert Tweedy in July 1936. The couple had a son and two daughters and settled in Stillorgan in Dublin.

The poverty and malnutrition suffered by many in Ireland during the Second World War had a profound impact on her. She was moved to take political action after seeing the grinding poverty of Dublin tenement life laid bare in *Marrowbone Lane*, a play by Robert Collis revived at the Gate Theatre in 1941.

With Andrée Sheehy-Skeffington and several friends, she organised a petition in May 1941 calling for the introduction of rationing to ensure fair distribution of food and fuel. This led, the following year, to the development of the Irish Housewives Association (IHA), a non-denominational pressure group focused on a broad range of interests, including school meals, hygiene regulations and consumer issues.

Hilda was also an early advocate of recycling and, as early as 1942, called for the development of paper and glass recycling facilities.

The members of the group weren't afraid to court controversy, and they attracted the wrath of Catholic newspapers, the clergy and some members of the public. The IHA supported the women laundry workers' strike in 1945, which won the introduction of paid holidays for all, and Dr Noel

Hilda's 1992 history of the Irish Housewives Association *A Link In The Chain* and Alan Hayes' book chronicling the Association

'Hilda was an early advocate of recycling and, as early as 1942, called for the development of paper and glass recycling facilities'

Browne's Mother and Child Scheme. They also campaigned for equal pay for women, the introduction of women police and the removal of the public service marriage bar.

The group became affiliated to the International Alliance of Women in 1947 and, later, was instrumental in setting up the Council for the Status of Women in 1973.

Meanwhile, in her working life, Hilda returned to Alexandra College to teach mathematics in the 1950s. The following decade, she and her husband opened the renowned children's shop Nimble Fingers, which stocks educational toys and equipment.

In 1990, Hilda received an honorary doctorate in laws from Trinity College Dublin and, two years later, she wrote a well-received history of the Association *A Link in the Chain*, musing: "Who would have thought in 1942 that women could move from the kitchen to Áras an Uachtaráin?"

She presented her papers to the National Archive in 2003.

Hilda died on 4 July 2005, and in 2009, her daughter Jean established the Hilda and Robert Tweedy biennial lecture series in Trinity College to honour their commitment to peace, gender and human rights and environmental issues.

RW

Maureen O'Carroll

(1913-1984)

Social activist and first female TD to hold position of party Chief Whip

Secretary, Lower Prices Council. Member of Administrative Council of the Labour Party and of the I.W.W.U. She is an Hon. Arts Graduate. As Secretary of the L.P.C. for seven years she has fought ceaselessly against High Prices and publicly opposed every increase. During the Milk Strike of 1953, fought for and succeeded in getting supplies of milk for sick babies and invalids.

When Maureen O'Carroll was asked whether she admired women who wanted to be as good as men, her reply was succinct and characteristic: "If I meet any woman who wants to be as good as a man, I'd say they lack ambition."

Maureen certainly didn't lack ambition. She might have been called 'Little Mo', but her small frame was the only thing that was diminutive about the mother of 11.

"After a conversation with her, you could walk on water and feel you could be anything you want

Printed with permission of John O'Carroll courtesy of Mná100

to be," her children said during a Newstalk documentary about the woman who inspired her son Brendan's hit TV show, Mrs Brown's Boys.

Julia Mary McHugh was born on 29 March, 1913, the eldest of Lizzie and Micheal's four children. Her parents had been planning to elope, but Lizzie's father came round to their romance and Michael sold the tickets he had bought to travel to America on board the *Titanic*. The policeman who bought them survived the fateful journey, but his wife did not.

Maureen's father, who was close to Michael Collins and very involved in Gaelic League circles, died when she was 11. His influence, however, lived on. As Maureen's daughter later said: "He led my mother to believe that she could do anything she wanted to do and be anything she wanted to be. Hence her amazing record in politics and social affairs."

Although Maureen studied in University College Galway as a novice nun, she later changed course. She became a language teacher and married cabinet-maker Gerard O'Carroll in July 1936.

The couple lived in Dublin and by the 1940s Maureen was already active in public life. She was a founding member of the Lower Prices Commission in 1947, set up to address rising prices and black marketeering after the Second World War.

In 1954, she was elected to Dáil Eireann as a Labour TD for Dublin North-Central, defeating the sitting Fianna Fáil TD Colm Gallagher. She worked as her party's chief whip, the first woman to hold that position in any Irish political party.

She was also instrumental in introducing the first female recruits to An Garda Síochána. Initially known as 'ban gardaí', or women guards, they faced sexism from many quarters. In 1958, a year before the first women joined the force, one TD told the Dáil that women would make a great addition as they had practice with a rolling-pin and might be just as able to wield a baton as a man.

'In 1958, a year before the first women joined An Garda Síochána, one TD told the Dáil that women would make a great addition as they had practice with a rolling-pin and might be just as able to wield a baton as a man'

Maureen O'Carroll tackled deeply ingrained prejudice too, and campaigned to have 'illegitimate' removed as a status from the birth certificates of children born to unmarried parents. She also vehemently opposed the illegal adoption of Irish children to the United States.

Her tenth child Brendan was born while she was a TD, and she adopted Phil, who was in a reform school, as a young child. When she faced bureaucracy about the adoption, she went all the way to the top – to the then Taoiseach Éamon de Valera – to overcome it.

Although she lost her Dáil seat in 1957, Maureen continued to contribute to public life and to campaign for social and economic change. She established a shelter for homeless women while working for Dublin City Council. When she died on 9 May, 1984, female gardaí formed a guard of honour at her funeral.

"The legacy she's left me," her son Brendan said, "is that every time I sit down to write Mrs Brown, I hear her voice."

RW

Maureen O'Carroll arriving at the High Court for the Batchelors Peas Case in 1954. She claimed the company had applied a false trade description to "specially selected marrowfats" containers as they contained a mixture of marrowfat and cheaper blue peas. Picture courtesy of the Irish Photo Archive

Máirín Hope

(1914-2009)

Architect, designer of playgrounds and nurseries, and campaigner for better facilities for pre-school children

When St Joseph's Day Nursery opened at the Coombe in Dublin in 1956, the *Irish Press* noted that the facility had grown "out of literally nothing". It was as if the Ladies Committee of the Civics Institute had created it from thin air because, as the paper went on to explain, its members had no money, no place to build and nothing to build it with.

What they had, however, was determination, resourcefulness and a belief that the Civics Institute, a philanthropic organisation, could make real improvements in people's lives with better town planning. The Institute's honorary secretary, architect Máirín Hope offered to design the centre free of charge, and the committee wrote hundreds of letters to secure the rest.

Soon, building contractors and providers pitched in to help, while Dublin Corporation gave the Institute a site at Maryland in the Coombe. A list of all the benefactors still hangs in the hall of St Joseph's.

In March 1956, the bright, colourful and child-centred nursery opened to provide affordable childcare for mothers who, as the

Máirín Hope at the drawing board with her daughters, l to r, Gabrielle, Cornelia and Caroline. Picture courtesy of Máirín's family

Saint Joseph's Nursery Centre

Photo by courtesy T P Gun

newspaper put it, had to "work in order to keep their families, or to supplement small earnings".

In a country that had enshrined in its Constitution the importance to the common good of having a woman stay at home, building a nursery to help working mothers was a bold step. The Civics Institute, however, was careful to stress that its work was designed to strengthen rather than weaken family life.

Nonetheless, St Joseph's, just like a similar nursery, St Brigid's, which had opened in Mountjoy Square in 1940, were "avant-garde for Ireland in that they introduced a new social infrastructure," as architectural and cultural historian Dr Ellen Rowley has observed.

Máirín Hope (née Cuffe) was born in Dublin and studied architecture at University College Dublin at a time when there were few women architects. She graduated in 1939 and married Alan Hope, a fellow architect, the same year. Their first project together was to design and self-build a house, which was inspired by one of the founders of modern architecture, Alvar Aalto.

'Meander', the family home designed and built in 1939 by Mairin and Alan Hope. Picture courtesy of her family. Picture courtesy of Máirín's family

The Second World War had made materials scarce so the couple used whatever was available to build 'Meander' in Foxrock, Dublin. Its external concrete block walls were clad with cedar boards while plywood sheets lined the interior. One of the upstairs windows was even fashioned from a glass door.

Alan Hope went on to work on many public commissions, while Máirín used her architectural training on pioneering projects aimed at improving the lives of people, and children in particular.

She designed sand-gardens, a sand-pit in St Stephen's Green, playgrounds and nurseries that put their users – children – at the centre of the design. In one letter to benefactors, Miss Keane, the Civics Institute secretary, gives a fascinating insight into how builders took to the idea with relish.

She wrote: "The workmen are wildly enthusiastic about everything. Not satisfied with the book measurements for fittings, they brought little children in and measured them to ensure correct heights for shelves."

Máirín explained the importance of supporting young children in a Sunday Independent interview: "It is known that 50 per cent of a child's potential intelligence is developed by the age of 4-and-a-half. Only 30 per cent is added between 4-8 years, and only another 20 is added between 8-16 years," she said.

Good design did not just apply to buildings either; it also applied to children's space outdoors. As founder, and first chairperson of, the Irish Pre-school Playgroups Association in 1969 (now known as Early Childhood Ireland), Máirín highlighted that point and said playgroups and playgrounds should be regulated and meet specific standards. To this end, the Civics Institute initiated and offered educational training and advocacy to those running playgroups to ensure they met professional standards in order to gain recognition and approval at government level.

She remained interested in pre-school education, social justice issues – she was a member of a Travellers' Support Group – and architecture for the rest of her life. One of her three daughters, Gabrielle, followed in her footsteps and qualified as an architect. In turn, two of her children, Ruth and Donal O'Herlihy, became architects too.

Ruth now lives in 'Meander', the house her grandmother built so many decades ago.

CF

Eileen Kennedy

(1914-1983)

Ireland's first woman judge and social reformer

Eileen Kennedy was one of six notable Irish women in an Irish school book *Firsts for Irish Women – They Led the Way*, published by Poolbeg Press in 2019 as part of their Heroes for Ireland series. Alongside former President Mary Robinson and Lilian Bland who was Ireland's first woman pilot, the country's first female judge took her rightful place.

While serving as Minister for Justice, Charles Haughey proposed Eileen Kennedy as the first woman member of the judiciary. He would later say that she "more than justified the confidence then placed in her, as her work in the Children's Court over the years testifies. Comprising a special blend of wisdom and compassion, her judgments were always fair, just and enlightened."

His views on Ireland's first woman district justice were echoed by Nuala Fennell, then Minister of State for Women's Affairs and Family Law Reform. After Eileen's death in 1983, she said Justice Kennedy "was known for her compassionate approach

Judge Eileen Kennedy. Picture courtesy of the *Sunday Independent*

LEGAL FIRSTS

On 1 November 1921, Frances Kyle BL and Averil Deverell BL made history in the new State when they became the first women to be called to the bar.

Averil Deverell. Picture by Liz Goldthorpe, courtesy of the Bar of Ireland

Frances Kyle. Picture courtesy of the School of Law, Trinity College Dublin

to cases with which she dealt, particularly during her years in the Children's Court".

Eileen Kennedy, who was born on 30 May 1914, was the fourth child of solicitor Patrick Kennedy and his wife Delia. The family had a strong legal background. Her two brothers John and James also worked as solicitors.

After studying at St Louis Convent in Carrickmacross in Co Monaghan, Eileen decided to become a nurse and did her training at St Vincent's Hospital in Dublin. She qualified in 1934 and worked as a registered general nurse, serving in the Irish Army nursing service for three years during the Second World War. In 1943, she left the profession to study law and, as a qualified solicitor, she joined her father's practice.

In April 1964, she was appointed district justice in the Republic of Ireland, the first woman to hold the position. She was also the first Justice to appear with their head uncovered.

Judge Mary Kotsonouris, at the time a solicitor's apprentice, said there was a "frisson of excitement at such daring".

From the start of her career as a judge, Eileen was given particular responsibility for the Children's Court and, from 1967, she was attached permanently to it.

She was appointed chair of a committee in 1967 to report on the reformatory and industrial school systems. It was published three years later, and the results of the highly critical Kennedy Report were momentous for Irish society. The Department of Education was no longer in charge of childcare; instead, it came under the auspices of the Department of Health. Foster care and residential homes replaced industrial and reformatory schools.

The report also called for a new Children's Act, a measure that Eileen would campaign for throughout her life.

In April 1970, Eileen was appointed by Taoiseach Jack Lynch as a member of the first Commission on the Status of Women. Its report was instrumental in making important changes on the legal status of Irish women in relation to equal pay and removing the marriage bar.

Eileen was mugged in Dublin in February 1983. She fractured her hip and was forced to stay away from the courts for five months. Soon after returning to work, she had a heart attack while on holiday with her sister in Connemara. She died in Galway in October 1983. She had been due to retire the following May.

RW

Esther 'Ettie' Steinberg

(1914-1942)

Member of the Jewish community, seamstress and one of a handful Irish citizens murdered in the Holocaust

When Esther Steinberg was being deported with her husband and son to the Nazi death camp at Auschwitz in September 1942, she made one final, desperate attempt to alert her family in Dublin.

She wrote a coded message in Hebrew on a postcard and threw it from the window of a moving train, hoping it would somehow make its way to 28 Raymond Terrace, now part of the South Circular Road in the capital. She had moved there with her family as a young girl, attending the nearby school, St Catherine's in Donore Ave, and later training as a seamstress.

Her family spoke of her "golden hands" and of a dressmaker who showed exceptional skill and creativity.

Now, she wanted to tell her parents of the fate she sensed awaited her. She wrote: "Uncle Lechem, we did not find, but we found Uncle Tisha B'Av". 'Lechem' is the Hebrew word for bread while Tisha B'Av is a Jewish fast day commemorating the destruction of the temple. Her message meant: Instead of sustenance, we found destruction.

Ettie, her husband Wojteck and their baby son, Léon, were transported by train on 2 September 1942 from Drancy, outside Paris, to Auschwitz-Birkenau death camp where they were murdered in gas chambers two days later. Pictures courtesy of the Mémorial de la Shoah, Paris

'When she was being deported, Ettie wrote a coded message in Hebrew on a postcard and threw it from the window of a moving train, hoping it would somehow make its way to Dublin. Miraculously it did'

The postcard miraculously reached its destination and it would have been immediately understood. It was a particularly cruel blow because the family had finally managed to secure a visa for Ettie, her Belgian husband Wojteck Gluck and their toddler son Léon. It arrived in Toulouse a day after they were all deported.

The couple had married in the summer of 1937 at the Greenville Hall Synagogue, South Circular Road, Dublin. By then, Ettie had been in Dublin for more than a decade. She was born in the former Czechoslovakia on 11 January 1914 and moved to the city with her parents, Bertha Roth and Aaron Hirsch Steinberg, when she about 12 years old. She was one of seven children.

After she married, she moved to Antwerp where her husband worked in the family business. When it became clear that Jewish people were in danger, they sought refuge in Paris.

The couple's son Léon was born there in March 1939. Later that year, when the Second World War broke out, the threat of violence forced them to move again, and to keep moving for the next three years. They went from hiding place to hiding place in the south of France, staying in each place for just a few nights.

In the late summer of 1942, they were discovered and, with tens of thousands of Jewish people, rounded up and sent to Drancy transit camp outside Paris. On 2 September, at 8.55am,

Ettie Steinberg and Wojteck Gluck married in the summer of 1937 at the Greenville Hall Synagogue, South Circular Road, Dublin. Picture courtesy of the Irish Jewish Museum

Europe with their families. They were all murdered, along with members of their families. More Irish victims are coming to light as stories unfold.

For now, all six of those named will be honoured on 1 June 2022 with Stolpersteine, the small brass memorial plaques, or "stumbling stones", that have been laid in more than a thousand cities to honour the memory of those who died in the Holocaust.

CF

The Stolpersteine in memory of Ettie, Wojteck and Leon to be embedded in Dublin in June 2022. Picture by Jim Leonard, courtesy of Holocaust Education Trust Ireland

Ettie, her husband and son were deported. Each detail was noted in minute detail at the internment camp. They arrived in Auschwitz two days later. It is believed they were murdered immediately.

For many years, it was thought that Ettie Steinberg was the only Irish person to die in the Holocaust but in 2019, Dr David Jackson, a consultant statistician, discovered three others. He found evidence that Isaac Shishi, Ephraim Saks and his sister, Jeanne, or Lena, were born in Ireland before they returned to

Dr Sheila Tinney

(1918-2010)

Mathematician, theoretical physicist and accomplished pianist

In 1948, when Sheila Tinney took up a fellowship to work on nuclear physics at the Institute for Advanced Study in Princeton in the United States, Albert Einstein and Freeman Dyson were among her colleagues. Later, she would tell her students at University College Dublin (UCD) that she queued up for coffee with Einstein.

It is a measure of her pioneering work in the field that she was researching in the company of such luminaries. From an early age, her flair for mathematical science was evident. She was one of only eight girls – there were 128 boys – to take honours mathematics in the Leaving Certificate in 1935.

Her father Michael Power, a professor of mathematics at University College Galway, must have been an influence, but she also received support at her school, the Dominican College at Taylor's Hill in Galway and, later, at St Mary's Dominican Convent in Cabra, Dublin.

Even so, it was still unusual for women to study mathematical science at higher level in Ireland in the 1930s. Not only was

Portrait by artist Judith Henihan. Picture courtesy of the Dublin Institute for Advanced Studies

she one of the few women to do so, but she also excelled. She graduated top of her class with a first-class honours BA from UCD in 1938.

Sheila went on to complete an MA and won a scholarship to the University of Edinburgh in Scotland to work under the direction of Nobel laureate Max Born. In 1941, she was awarded a PhD for her research on the stability of crystals.

The same year, she was appointed assistant lecturer in mathematics at UCD and, four years later, she became a statutory lecturer. She was also a part-time fellow at the Dublin Institute for Advanced Studies. Its director, Erwin Schrödinger – the Nobel Prize-winning physicist whose famous cat experiment shone a light on quantum theory – said she was among "the best equipped and most successful of the younger generation of theoretical physicists in this country".

She collaborated with others, some of them Nobel laureates, and published several papers on subjects ranging from wave mechanics and cosmic radiation to crystal lattices and quantum electrodynamics.

Botanist Phyllis Clinch, Irish scholar Eleanor Knott, art historian Françoise Henry and Sheila Tinney, then still Power, were the first four female members of Royal Irish Academy, admitted in 1949.

In 1952, Sheila married Sean Tinney, an engineer, but she continued to work and was appointed Associate Professor in Mathematical Physics in UCD in 1966.

She had many other interests. She was a keen sportswoman, enjoying hill-walking, skiing, tennis and riding. While at Princeton in the late-40s, she sustained concussion when she was knocked off

Dr Sheila Tinney's children, Ethna, Hugh and Deirdre Tinney, with her portrait. Picture courtesy of the Dublin Institute for Advanced Studies

her horse who bolted after disturbing a rattlesnake. The experience didn't put her off, however. She was also an accomplished pianist like her mother, Christina, who died when Sheila was just 12. She said one of her fondest memories was of her mother playing at her childhood home in Galway.

Sheila and Sean Tinney had three children, Deirdre, Ethna, a concert pianist and radio and TV music producer, and Hugh, the internationally acclaimed pianist.

In 2019, a portrait of Sheila Tinney by Judith Henihan was unveiled at the Dublin Institute for Advanced Studies (DIAS). CEO and Registrar Dr Eucharia Meehan said she was "a truly remarkable scientist... she excelled in her field, both on a national and international level, and could count some of the most famous and influential minds in history as colleagues: whilst at DIAS, Erwin Schrödinger and Walter Heitler, and elsewhere, Albert Einstein and Freeman Dyson, to mention but a few."

At the unveiling, Sheila's son Hugh Tinney said: "We are very proud of our mother's legacy as a pioneering female scientist. We are delighted her portrait will hang permanently at DIAS, and we hope it inspires generations of future scientists to build on her scientific achievements."

CF

Dr Sheila Tinney (third from left) in 1942. Picture courtesy of the Royal Academy of Ireland

'She would tell her students at University College Dublin that she queued up for coffee with Albert Einstein when she took up a fellowship at the Institute for Advanced Study in Princeton in the United States'

Margaret Gaj

(1919-2011)

Restaurant-owner and activist

Former Taoiseach Garret FitzGerald famously described Margaret Gaj's restaurant on Baggot Street in Dublin as the "place everyone was either going to or coming from".

It was a hub of constant activity with a wide-ranging clientele that took in the broadest cross section of Dublin society. As one of those customers, writer and early feminist Rosita Sweetman, put it: "Trade unionists, aristocrats, lawyers, bank robbers, prostitutes, students, artists, prisoners, civil-rights activists and Women's Libbers all rubbed shoulders around the scrubbed hardwood tables."

The food was simple, homely and cheap. Those couldn't afford to pay for it, didn't, and like everyone they were served one of the staples, goulash or and pineapple on toast with pots of proper tea.

In 1965, an advert in Trinity News offered this guide to the uninitiated: "Pronounce it "Guy/Spell Find it 132 Lower Baggot Street". The ad also promised "excellent meals at very reasonable prices",

Margaret Gaj. Photo by Derek Speirs

At Gaj's Restaurant, Lower Baggot Street. (on the right of frame) Margaret Gaj with Frank Crummy. Pictures courtesy of Derek Speirs

Ad from Trinty News

gained renown not so much as a restaurant but as a meeting place to discuss what were often considered subversive views at that time.

In the 1970s, it became the crucible for the social activism that gave birth to the Irish Women's Liberation Movement with Margaret Gaj herself acting as treasurer.

In 1971, the movement published Chains or Change, a manifesto listing the many obstacles faced by women in Irish society.

The marriage bar was in force, which meant women had to leave their jobs in the public sector once they got married. There was no contraception, no divorce and no legal or financial independence. Several of the women active in that movement were regulars at Gaj's – Máirín de Burca, Mary Kenny, Mary Maher, Nell McCaffery and Rosita Sweetman among them.

The owner of Gaj's restaurant took a back seat, though. Born in Scotland to Irish parents in Edinburgh, Scotland, in 1919, Margaret Gaj (née Dunlop) always felt Irish. "You could not be a Catholic in Scotland without feeling it," she said in a newspaper interview.

She moved to Dublin with her Polish husband Boleslaw Gaj in the 1940s. The couple met during the Second World War. She was a Red Cross nurse and he was a patient at a hospital in Stirling.

They became Irish citizens and invested money Margaret had inherited from an uncle in a farm in Wicklow, and later a café.

Pictured at the launch of 'Monday at Gaj's' by Anne Stopper are author Anne Stopper, Mrs Gaj, Mary Sheerin, Mairin Johnston and Marie McMahon (sitting). Picture courtesy of Derek Speirs

Pictured at the launch of 'Monday at Gaj's' by Anne Stopper are (standing)- Emer Philbin Bowman, Rosita Sweetman, Mairin de Burca, Mary Sheerin, Mairin Johnston and (sitting) Roisin Callender, Mrs. Gaj, Marie McMahon. Picture courtesy of Derek Speirs

Both were ultimately unsuccessful, but she did succeed in setting up a branch of the Irish Countrywomen's Association in Baltinglass in 1954 before moving to Dublin.

She opened a restaurant in Molesworth Street and moved to 132 Lower Baggott Street in the mid-60s to open the famous Gaj's. If it was a centre of political discussion, it took its cue from its owner Margaret Gaj. Mrs Gaj, as she was known, was "formidable, kind and absolutely fearless in taking on the establishment", according to journalist Mary Maher.

She joined the Labour Party, though didn't stay and was deeply involved in campaigns for better housing and for prisoners' rights. She also campaigned against corporal punishment.

She was known for her sharp tongue, but that was offset by her kindness and determination to help those in need. She ran regular fundraisers and more than once provided bail money when activists were arrested.

The restaurant closed in 1980 and its passing was noted – and mourned – in the national newspapers. Margaret Gaj left a note on the door thanking customers and saying that it was not easy to be a socialist in a capitalist society.

All the same, she left her mark.

CF

Prof Ethna Gaffney

(1920-2011)

First woman professor at the Royal College of Surgeons in Ireland

Remembered by her daughter Phyllis Gaffney

Fate and fortune combined to produce the first woman professor in Dublin's Royal College of Surgeons (RCSI). Suddenly widowed at 31, during her fourth pregnancy, while still grieving the accidental death of her eldest child, she was made breadwinner by necessity, not design. Her education and previous employment gave her the resources to face what had to be faced.

Ethna O'Malley was born into a privileged Galway family in 1920 and enjoyed a sunny upbringing as the third among eight children: swimming, tennis, party-going, reading, fruit-picking. Educated by the Dominicans and then at Loreto Abbey Rathfarnham, she opted for science in University College Galway because she had never studied it before and – more importantly – science had the shortest registration queue. (No career guidance back then.)

Scholarships and prizes led to a doctorate in biochemistry with University College Dublin's E.J. Conway, a singular achievement for an Irish woman in 1945.

Prof Ethna Gaffney opted for science in University College Galway because she had never studied it before and – more importantly – science had the shortest registration queue. (No career guidance back then)

She was immediately hired to launch a pioneering Diploma in Dietetics in the College of Science, Cathal Brugha Street. This involved lectures on chemistry, biochemistry, physiology, bacteriology and health nutrition. Her students were women; science was new to them all. In the hospitals where they did work placements, older medics were deeply suspicious of dietetics.

Ethna resigned her job after marriage in 1947 to Jim Gaffney, a Trinity College pathologist who had worked in the Irish Red Cross hospital set up after the Second World War in the bombed-out ruins of Saint-Lô in Normandy.

154

Pregnancies came in quick succession: three sons and another child on the way, when tragedy struck. Twice. In October 1951, their three-year-old, Patrick, was drowned. In January 1952, Jim was on the first Aer Lingus plane to crash, in Snowdonia. Aged 38, he was returning from a Cambridge pathology conference.

These accidental deaths – one as old as time (children playing near water), one new (the miracle of aviation) – were catastrophic. Two months later, Ethna's premature daughter, severely underweight, was rushed from Galway to an incubator in Dublin's Temple Street, to prevent a third tragedy. I was that baby.

Ethna got a fellowship with Vincent Barry's team at the Medical Research Council before moving (1954) to lecture in Surgeons, where she remained until her retirement in 1987. This was rewarding work: she helped to train doctors from around the globe, from Norway to Nigeria, China to Canada, Singapore to Sierra Leone. Student yearbooks record a larger-than-life enthusiast who swept into the lecture hall, talking fast.

In a solidly male world, she was proud of her promotion to professor. "My most memorable occasion in College was surely one night in 1962, shortly after I had been appointed Professor of Chemistry," she later recalled. "That January, I received an invitation to the conferring of the honorary Fellowship on President Éamon de Valera and to the formal dinner afterwards. The dinner was attended by the other professors and members of Council. About 60 people sat down to eat; all of them were men, except myself. Wives and consorts were not asked, so there was no competition whatsoever."

Combining lone parenting and a demanding job was difficult with three small children, particularly in Ireland of the 1950s and '60s. How did she cope? She had essential home help, solid family support, close friends, and she drew on latent resilience and strength of character. Life was seasonal, and in the summer she gladly gave time to mothering. Once the June examination scripts were marked and meetings over, there was the annual exodus of the black Morris Minor to her parents' place in Galway.

Work-life balance remains a perennial challenge for lone parents, perhaps even more in today's academic world. Under less pressure to meet research targets, my mother availed of the holidays to prepare new lectures, recharge batteries and bond with her children.

In her prime she was adventurous, resourceful and energetic. A strong swimmer, she played golf, loved travelling, gardening, friends, parties, and believed in the power of education to transform lives. She sometimes regretted not having studied medicine. Had the science queue been longer, she might well have done exactly that.

After getting her doctorate in biochemistry, Ethna Gaffney was hired to launch a pioneering Diploma in Dietetics in the College of Science, Cathal Brugha Street

'About 60 people sat down to eat; all of them were men, except myself. Wives and consorts were not asked, so there was no competition whatsoever'

Pictures courtesy of
Ethna's daughter Phyllis Gaffney

Activists at Connolly Station, Dublin, in 1971 getting ready to board the train to Belfast to buy contraceptives.
Picture by Eddie Kelly, courtesy of the *Irish Times*

milestones

1951 Health Minister Dr Noel Browne of Clann na Poblachta proposes free maternal care for all mothers and babies. Seen as interference in the family, the measure is opposed by the Irish Medical Association and the Catholic Bishops. Minister Browne resigns, but he is later re-elected as an Independent TD.

1957 The Married Women Status Act gives women the separate right to own property.

1959 The first 12 female Garda recruits are sworn in (*see entry on Maureen O'Carroll*).

1960 *Country Girls* by Edna O'Brien is banned in Ireland because it contains sexually explicit material.

1969 The Irish Family Planning Association is founded.

1971 Some 49 members of the Irish Women's Liberation Movement defy customs to illegally import contraceptives to Dublin from Belfast on the famous 'contraception' train. Arriving back at Connolly Station laden with condoms and spermicides, they refused to hand over their contraband. Their bold action attracted international publicity and drew attention to the campaign to lift restrictions on the sale of contraceptives.

1973 The Council for the Status of Women is founded to help gain equality for women. Hilda Tweedy of the Irish Housewives' Association chairs it (*see entry on Hilda Tweedy*).

1973 The marriage bar is removed. In the same year, the Report of the Commission on the Status of Women is published. It identifies 49 discriminations against women to be removed.

1977 The Employment Equality Act is passed.

1979 Women Today, presented by Marian Finucane (*see entry on Marian Finucane*), is first aired on RTÉ Radio to discuss issues affecting women.

Frankie 'Frances' Byrne

(1921-1993)

Broadcaster, pioneering businesswoman and agony aunt

Frankie Byrne started each episode of her hugely popular radio show 'Woman's Page' – or 'Dear Frankie' as it was popularly known – in the same way: "The problems I will be discussing today may not be yours, but they could be some day," she said in a distinctive, lived-in voice that is still recalled today.

When first broadcast on Radio Éireann in 1963, the daily lunchtime broadcast was intended as a home management programme to suit sponsors Jacob's Biscuits. Frankie Byrne, however, had no interest in the domestic sphere and the programme soon developed into a taboo-breaking discussion of the nation's problems, casting her as national 'agony aunt' in the process.

She took to the role with relish, dispensing forthright advice to the hundreds of women, and often men, who confided in her. To one listener who complained her fiancé wanted to move from the city to the country, she had this to say: "If you love him, you'd live on a mountainside with him, but if you blackmail him into your way of thinking you may never know a day's happiness."

She received more than 5,000 letters from women and men seeking advice on love, life and heartache. Photograph courtesy of RTÉ Archives

158

And to the 30-year-old male executive having difficulty finding a girl who would "meet his standards", she delivered these memorable lines: "This may come as a shock to you, but women are actually human beings... I suspect the man who is looking for a nice, settled girl is really searching for an unpaid housekeeper with a civil tongue in her head."

The only artist she played on the show was Frank Sinatra, a man who had a number to suit every occasion, she once said, although she didn't get to see him when he performed in Dublin in 1989.

During the show's run from 1963-1985, Frankie Byrne responded to more than 5,000 letters on a range of issues that reflected a changing Ireland. While the truth about domestic violence and child abuse remained unspoken, the once-taboo topics of contraception and relationships, in all their forms, were aired more openly from the 1980s onwards.

If Frankie Byrne's radio show reflected the changes taking place in Ireland, her own career path did too. She set up her own public relations company, Frankie Byrne Ltd, in 1963 drawing on the contacts she had made as a secretary in the Brazilian consulate and later at McConnells advertising agency.

Her nascent company got off to an exceptional start with a deal to handle the publicity during US President John F. Kennedy's visit to Ireland. She was also involved in setting up the annual Jacob's Awards, the first Irish television awards. A colleague from that time remembers Frankie as a woman who

Broadcaster, author and harpist Kathleen Watkins with her husband, veteran broadcaster Gay Byrne, and Frankie Byrne at the *Jacob's Television Awards* Frankie helped to establish. Photograph courtesy of RTÉ Archives

'This may come as a shock to you, but women are actually human beings... I suspect the man who is looking for a nice, settled girl is really searching for an unpaid housekeeper with a civil tongue in her head'

went out of her way to help others, particularly those she felt needed support.

What few knew, however, was that the nation's most famous agony aunt had her own heartache. She had a long-term relationship with fellow broadcaster Frank Hall and became pregnant in the 1950s. Single women at the time had few, if any, options and the vast majority, like Frankie, gave up their children for adoption.

She later met her daughter and they had a relationship for a number of years, although it was not always a straightforward one. Speaking in 2012, her daughter said: "I suppose it's a slightly manufactured relationship as well, and lots of things came into play."

Frankie Byrne died in 1993, but her name still conjures up the radio show that acted as the soundtrack to many an Irish childhood.

CF

Sybil Connolly

(1921-1998)

Acclaimed Fashion Designer

Sybil Connolly said it in her own inimitable style: "I like to buy my mink and diamonds myself". She was well able to do so; at the peak of her success in the 1950s, the fashion designer was earning over $500,000 in gross sales.

She was the first Irish woman to make a splash on the international fashion stage, wowing Hollywood stars and US socialites alike. Among the clients who wore her signature crochet, tweed and lace creations were actresses such as Elizabeth Taylor, Julie Andrews and Rosalind Russell.

When First Lady Jacqueline Kennedy sat for her official White House portrait, she wore one of Sybil's characteristic pleated linen dresses.

Sybil was born in Wales in 1921, the elder of John and Evelyn Connolly's two daughters. She moved to Waterford as a teenager with her mother after her Irish father died.

From a young age, Sybil was interested in fashion and at 17 moved to London where she was employed as an apprentice

Acclaimed fashion designer Sybil Connolly:
'I like to buy my mink and diamonds myself'
Illustration by Holly Christine Callaghan

dressmaker at Bradley's, a prestigious Irish firm. After the outbreak of the Second World War, she returned to Ireland and worked as a buyer for the Richard Alan fashion house.

When the company's chief designer left suddenly in 1952, she stepped into his shoes with aplomb. Her designs boasted a distinctly Irish twist, and her innovative use of traditional fabrics brought her to the attention of the influential Carmel Snow, then editor of *Harper's Bazaar*.

Her big break would come in 1953 when Snow brought several US buyers and members of the press to Ireland to see Sybil's collections at a show in Dunsany Castle in Co Meath.

One of Sybil's designs, a full-length red cape and a white crochet dress, made the front cover of Life magazine in the US, under the caption, "Irish Invade Fashion World"

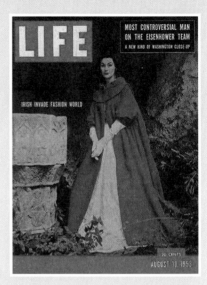

Later that year, a full-length red cape and a white crochet dress she had designed appeared on the front cover of *Life* magazine. It was captioned 'Irish Invade Fashion World' and Sybil's name became synonymous with style.

In 1957, she launched her own couture line and moved into 71 Merrion Square in Dublin, which she referred to as "the house that linen built".

A passionate advocate for this country, she said: "I feel that as long as we can show such beauty in design and texture as we do in our Irish cottage industries, we cannot ever be called a vanishing race."

During this time, Sybil, who had been described as Ireland's

Sybil Connolly. Pictures from the Sybil Connolly Collection, courtesy of the Hunt Museum

'BLUEBIRD'

IRISH LACE

PLEATED LINEN

Bluebird design sketch. Picture from Sybil Connolly Collection, courtesy of the Hunt Museum

'When First Lady Jacqueline Kennedy sat for her official White House portrait, she wore one of Sybil's characteristic pleated linen dresses'

A very religious woman, Sybil asked a priest to bless each collection before its presentation.

According to a February 1959 review in the *New York Times*, her latest collection "showed tweeds, as she always has and always will". This review would prove to be accurate. Sybil was certain that "good fashion did not need to change".

She ignored the 1960s trend of mini-skirts and hated trousers, questioning why someone would "set out to deliberately make themselves look so awful".

As the decades passed and fashions became increasingly contemporary, Sybil became interested in interior decoration. She refurbished the 18th-century Swiss Cottage in Cahir, designed tableware for Tiffany & Co and glass for Tipperary Crystal. She also wrote, and collaborated on, a number of books on Irish homes and gardens.

After her death in May 1998, thousands of people visited 71 Merrion Square to bid on the house contents in an auction of 600 lots. Her portrait hangs in the National Gallery in Dublin and some of her archives and clothes are on display at the Hunt Museum in Limerick.

RW

best unofficial ambassador by New York-based fashion publicist Eleanor Lambert, was able to directly employ over 100 women working as weavers and lace-makers.

Brigid Mary Cotter

(1921-1978)

Renowned chemist and barrister

Brigid Mary Cotter not only had a multi-faceted career in many areas of chemistry, she also trained as a barrister in later life. She was 51 when she was called to the Irish bar in 1972 after studying for several years at the University of London.

Brigid, born in Roscommon in January 1921, was the eldest of Nicholas and Bridie's 12 children. Nicholas was the chief agricultural officer for the county and, later in her career, she followed in her father's footsteps to become an agricultural inspector for the Irish Government.

She studied at the Convent of Mercy in Roscommon followed by the Ursuline Convent in Sligo. After school, she went to University College Dublin (UCD) and graduated with a Bachelor of Science in chemistry and mathematics in 1944.

The following year, Brigid was awarded a Master's of Science in recognition of her work on epanorin, a chemical constituent of the lichen Lecanora epanora. She remained in UCD for another year working as a demonstrator in chemistry.

Brigid Mary Cotter from *The Irish Press*, 1972

from The Irish Press, 1972

Miss Brigid M. Cotter, Ranelagh, Dublin, and Miss Jane Flood, Rathgar, Dublin, the only girl students called to the Bar yesterday.

'Brigid was appointed chief technical officer in charge of the butter-testing station of the Department of Agriculture'

At the same time, Brigid was also involved with the Medical Research Council working on atmospheric pollution in Dublin. Then, as now, environmental concerns sparked public debate. In the 1930s, the Irish Government tried to boost the use of Irish turf as a home-heating fuel as it emitted fewer toxins than the coal imported from Britain. The only thing that significantly reduced the use of coal, however, was the Second World War which stopped all coal imports. As a result, air quality had improved by the mid-1940s.

Around this time, Brigid graduated with diplomas in both bacteriology and food technology and then moved to England to develop her career. In 1947, she got a job at the Imperial Chemical Industries laboratories in Manchester where her area of specialisation was moulds and fungi, such as penicillin.

When she returned to Ireland in 1948, she taught in Coláiste Íde, a girls' boarding school in Dingle, Co Kerry, which is based on the former estate of Lord Ventry. A year later, she changed direction and worked as a chemist in the State laboratory in Dublin for 10 years, four of which were spent in charge of the bacteriological section.

After she became an agricultural inspector in 1958, Brigid was appointed chief technical officer in charge of the butter-testing station of the Department of Agriculture.

While she held the latter post for the rest of her life, she continued to expand her interests and began a course of extra-mural law studies at the University of London. A diligent student, she was awarded a Bachelor of Laws in 1963 and a Master of Laws in 1969.

Mary (far left) was called to the Irish bar in 1972. Picture courtesy of the Bar of Ireland

As a result of these studies, she was called to the English bar and later to the Irish bar. Brigid was a keen member of law committees and even travelled as far as Sydney, Australia, to attend meetings of the International Bar Council.

A member of the Royal Dublin Society (RDS) and a fellow of the Institute of Chemists of Ireland, Brigid was also an enthusiastic bee-keeper in her spare time. *The Irish Beekeeper* journal recalled

her "able advice" and said she gave assistance at all times.

She died in Dublin on 20 November 1978, aged 57. Her legacy lives on as she funded the prestigious Brigid Cotter Prize which is awarded to external law students of her alma mater, the University of London.

RW

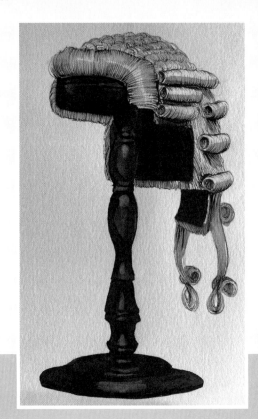

Pearl Phelan
Sr Joseph Ignatius
(1921-2010)
Head of theatre nursing and hospice-care pioneer

When Abba played their only gig in Dublin in 1979, crowds flocked to the Gresham Hotel in the city centre to try to catch a glimpse of the superstars. Tickets to their RDS concert were hard to get and the price was pushed up by touts selling on the black market.

At the time, Pearl Phelan/Sr Joseph Ignatius had a teenage Abba fan, desperate to go to the concert, in her care at Our Lady's Hospice in Harold's Cross. Sr Ignatius thought Abba was a man and rang the Gresham asking to speak to him. In any event, she got through and secured her patient a front-row ticket.

Her great-niece, author Liz Nugent, tells the story as an illustration of the kindness and resourcefulness of a woman who was a pioneer in the development of end-of-life and palliative care in Ireland. Sr Ignatius, known to many as 'Pearl' or 'Aunt Pearl', also set up the hospice home-care service, facilitating pain-managed, end-of-life care in patients' own homes.

In 1987, her work was acknowledged with a Rehab People of the Year award which she received with fellow hospice advocate, Sister Francis Rose O'Flynn. The judges described their work at Our Lady's Hospice as "a modern-day miracle".

In an interview earlier that year, Sr Ignatius told the *Evening Herald*: "If you can try to enable each person to live life to the full, control their symptoms so that they are freed from pain and the fear of pain, you come close to achieving the aim of the hospice."

Born in 1921 in Clonmel, Co Tipperary, to John Bernard and Mary Agnes Phelan, she was the third of six children. She and her sisters Kitty, Maura and Ellie and surviving brother Michael (their brother John died when he was 10) were orphaned when Pearl was just 13. Already close, this early loss fostered in Pearl a lifelong closeness with, and devotion to, her siblings.

She went on to train and work as a nurse before entering the Irish Sisters of Charity in Dublin as a novice at the relatively late age of 31.

As head of theatre nursing in St Vincent's Hospital on St Stephen's Green, Dublin, she oversaw the hospital's move to its new location in Elm Park in 1970, before being transferred by her Mother Superior to Our Lady's Hospice in Harold's Cross.

There, she successfully lobbied the Department of Health for funding to extend and modernise the building. She constantly worked to improve patient care and travelled to the UK and America to study best practice.

In the mid-70s, she went to Hackney in the UK to learn more about the latest developments in palliative care and terminal pain

The miracle worker

DES NIX meets SISTER IGNATIUS PHELAN who works with the dying in Our Lady's Hospice in Harold's Cross

A Person of the Year, Sister Ignatius of Our Lady's Hospice, Harold's Cross.   Picture by Cyril Byrne.

Newspaper article - *The Sunday Press*, November 29th, 1987

'Her leadership style and skill were best summed up by Chinese philosopher, Lao Tzu, who said: "As for the best leaders – the people do not notice their existence"'
- her nephew, John Blake Dillon

management. The founder of the hospice movement there, Dame Cicely Saunders, became a friend and valued mentor.

When Pearl died in 2010, her nephew John Blake Dillon recalled a woman who had four families – her physical family, her religious community, the hospice and the families of those she helped to negotiate a path through terminal illness and bereavement. He said her leadership style and skill were best summed up by Chinese philosopher, Lao Tzu, who said: "As for the best leaders – the people do not notice their existence."

Film-maker Alan Gilsenan, who made *The Hospice* documentary series at St Francis Hospice in Raheny, Dublin, recalled how his mother *"went to Pearl"*, her childhood friend, for the last two weeks of her life. He said it was very reassuring to know she was in safe hands and wrote of the *"comfort of complete competence, the assurance of dignity and respect [and], a strong sense of sheer goodness, even"*.

CF

All pictures courtesy of Pearl's family

Pearl with her family

Máire Mhac an tSaoi

(1922-2021)

Groundbreaking poet, barrister and diplomat

When Máire Mhac an tSaoi died, mourners heard that the mystery and miracle of this singular poet was that she was a middle-class Dublin woman who had emerged as the "standard-bearer" for the language and literature of rural Gaeltacht life.

She was formed by the Munster Gaeltacht, she said in one interview, explaining how frequent and long stays in Dún Chaoin had immersed her in the language and life of West Kerry. That early experience gave her a medium to voice the intimate lives of women in an open and frank way and, as fellow poet Nuala Ní Dhomhnaill put it, she dragged "Irish-language poetry kicking and screaming into the 20th century".

She paved the way for others too, such as Eavan Boland (see entry on Eavan Boland) and, in the process, became one of the finest Irish poets of the 20th century in both Irish and English.

Máire Mac an tSaoi also excelled in many other fields. She was a critic, scholar, translator, barrister and diplomat. She was one of the first women diplomats appointed by the Department

Máire Mhac an tSaoi. Picture courtesy of O'Brien Press

Máire's autobiography *The Same Age As The State*

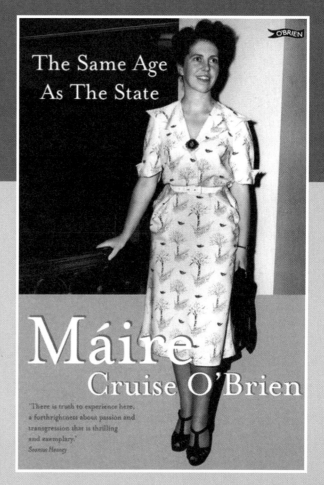

The Same Age As The State

Máire Cruise O'Brien

'There is truth to experience here, a forthrightness about passion and transgression that is thrilling and exemplary.'
Seamus Heaney

of External Affairs in 1947 and travelled to Franco's Spain, the Council of Europe in Strasbourg and the United Nations General Assembly in New York.

And she was a life-long promoter of women's rights, as Cllr Damian O'Farrell recounts after personally bearing witness to what he describes as her "brave feminism".

"As a young teen," he recalls, "I attended Mass in St Fintan's Church, Sutton. Each year, without fail, on Vocation Sunday during the priest's speech and request for vocations, she would stand up at her seat in the body of the church and call out: 'Father, Father, what about women priests?'"

She repeated the questions once or twice, politely, but was always ignored by the priest who went on speaking. She sat down, recalls Cllr Farrell, "usually at the behest of her two mortified children [Patrick and Margaret]".

Máire Mhac an tSaoi was born in Dublin into a political family in April 1922. Both parents had been active in the Easter Rising of 1916; her mother Margaret Browne, a teacher, acted as a

Two of Máire's extensive catalogue of publications

courier while her father Seán MacEntee, later a Fianna Fáil Tánaiste and minister, fought in the GPO. After they married, her mother was the family breadwinner and she was enraged about measures in the 1937 Constitution that relegated women to the domestic sphere.

In 2015, Máire recalled a "really big row" at home: "My mother, who had carried the finances of the family all the way since 1922, while my father earned hardly anything, was furious. She couldn't bring herself to talk to him."

It was Margaret Browne who taught her daughter Latin at the age of six. She also set the irregular French verbs to music "for chanting and skipping along the roads to", as Máire once put it. That early schooling in language led her to study a joint degree in Celtic studies and modern languages in University College Dublin.

She had several qualifications – diplomacy, law, translation – but it is her poetry that stands out. She published five collections from 1956 to 1999 in Irish, a language she said was vital to Ireland as "the prime catalyst in the creation of a truly European culture".

When she married diplomat Conor Cruise O'Brien in 1962, her father felt she was wasting her education. However, she continued to write, winning many accolades and plaudits. In 1968, she was already being described as "a major Irish-language poet", a distinction that lives on after the death of this exceptional woman who was the same age as the State, as her autobiography noted.

CF

Agnes Bernelle

(1923-1999)

Singer, actress, theatre founder and secret wartime operative

Remembered by her granddaughter Leah Leslie

At 13, Agnes Bernelle, the daughter of a Jewish-Hungarian theatre owner and Protestant nanny, fled Nazi-regime Berlin for London where she broadcast under the codename 'Vicki' on a black propaganda radio-show designed to spread disinformation and cause confusion in wartime Germany.

She sent coded messages to the Resistance and once famously caused chaos in the German postal system by convincing German citizens to post samples of their poo in jars to their local Gestapo for 'Aryan health checks'.

Throughout her lifetime, Agnes acted in several films with headlining actors such as Vivien Leigh and Sean Connery. In 1956, she became the first non-stationary nude to appear on stage in London when she performed the dance of the seven veils as Salome.

While in London, Agnes fell in love with Desmond Leslie, a handsome Anglo-Irish spitfire pilot, and cousin of Winston Churchill. They got married in August 1945 and moved to Desmond's ancestral

Agnes Bernelle broadcast under the codename 'Vicki' on a black propaganda radio-show designed to spread disinformation in wartime Germany. All pictures courtesy of her family

castle in Co Monaghan, Ireland. Their marriage sounds like the stuff of fairy tales, but the reality was that Desmond was chronically unfaithful. When their marriage eventually imploded, a devastated but ever-resilient Agnes moved to Dublin, where she met the historian and author Maurice Craig, with whom she lived out the rest of her days.

She is known for having brought a slice of Weimar culture to Dublin, with her cabaret and interpretations of German composer Kurt Weill and theatre pioneer Bertolt Brecht. She was instrumental in setting up the Project Arts Theatre in Dublin, where she was its creative director. She sang live with Marc Almond, Elvis Costello, Tom Waits and Irish punk rock band, The Radiators.

Desmond & Agnes on
their wedding day in 1945

To me, she was my grandmother Aggie.

Even as a child, I was aware that she was quite different from other people's grandmothers. She dressed in a dramatic silhouette (to match her equally theatrical personality), always in black, adorned in faux jewels, occasionally donning red lipstick, a feather boa and a cigarette holder.

I remember simultaneously loving and being frightened of her, as she spoke in a husky, vibrating voice similar to that of a Disney villain. She always referred to everyone as 'Darling' in an accent that belonged to another era. I recall exploring her bedroom, covered in trinkets and treasures left over from her privileged yesteryears in pre-war Berlin. There was also a curtain down the centre of the bed that she shared with Maurice, which she would draw between them whenever she was cross with him.

Broadcasting in London in 1943

Agnes in the 1950 film
Stranger at my Door

174

Drama had a habit of finding Aggie, and she was known for taking in helpless strangers with tragic sob stories and championing social causes. These events often occurred at the expense and neglect of her own responsibilities, but at the core of her actions almost always lay very good intentions.

Like so many of that generation, Aggie was fierce in the face of death. When told that she had only six months left to live, she simply refused to pay any attention to her predicament, and continued to live on for another four years.

She remained passionately dedicated to performing until the very end. In those final few days, she received a call at the hospice asking if she would be available to perform her set the following month, to which she whimsically replied, *"That sounds wonderful Darling, and I'd absolutely love to, but I'll be dead by then!"*

Recently, my music library shuffled randomly and my grandmother's voice began to warble out an anti-Nazi cabaret song: *"The worries of this world are crushing you/ And yet this earth is such a friendly star/ Come tell me what it is that's bothering you..."* How much I wish I could, Granny.

'She sent coded messages to the Resistance and once famously caused chaos in the German postal system by convincing German citizens to post samples of their poo in jars to their local Gestapo for 'Aryan health checks''

Agnes and Maurice

1951

1926: My Jewish great grandfather Rudie Bernaur and grandmother Agnes Bernelle

Agnes (far left) and actress Marlene Dietrich

1953: Agnes with her sons Sean and Mark

Pictures: courtesy of Agnes Bernelle's family

175

Kay Mills

(1923-1996)

One of the greatest Gaelic players in history

"You know what to do, go out and keep at it." These were the words Kay Mills used to motivate her camogie team. And they worked. She spurred her teammates on to many victories over the years and, in the process, won a record 15 senior All-Ireland medals herself, the most won by any player in any code.

Kay, also known as the 'Inchicore Invincible', was awarded her last medal on her 38th birthday, the day she retired from her beloved sport.

She was born on 8 October 1923, to Thomas and Winifred Mills. Her mother died when she was 18 months old. Kay and her three siblings were raised by her maternal grandmother Charlotte, who like Thomas and Winifred, lived in Inchicore in Dublin.

Thomas Mills worked for Great Southern Railways (later part of CIÉ) which enabled Kay to use the company's sports club (Great Southern Railway Club - GSRC) thanks to the two pence a week deducted from her father's wages.

Kay Mills illustration by Holly Christine Callaghan.
Inset: Betty 'Gerry' Hughes let Kay hold the cup in 1961 after her last game

● Tommy Moore displays his Gaelic All Stars Award at last night's presentation of awards in Dublin last night. Admiring the trophy are Seamus Ryan, president of the G.A.A. (left), Mrs. G. Hill (Kathleen Mills) and Sean O'Siochain, general secretary, G.A.A.

'At customs in Dun Laoghaire, they told her she could keep the crockery but not the newspaper it was wrapped in, as the News of the World was one of many publications banned in Ireland at the time'

Sports Star of the Week in the Irish Press following Kay's last All-Ireland Final appearance

Kathleen Mills

SPORT STAR OF THE WEEK

Kathleen Mills, who won her fifteenth All-Ireland camogie medal on Sunday last when, in her last appearance, she played a big part in Dublin's victory over Tipperary by 7-2 to 4-1.

Always sporty, Kay took part in athletics, table tennis and gymnastics with the club, but camogie was her true love. She was five years old when she first held a hurley stick. "From that day to 1961, I never left it out of my hand… Camogie was my whole life," she said.

Aged 14 and after a single match, Kay was called up to wear the wine, green and white colours of GSRC's senior panel.

Only two years passed before she made her Dublin senior debut in 1941. Her position was left wing midfield, no 8, and it would remain hers alone for the next two decades.

Dublin beat Cork 4-1 to 2-2 in a replay in 1942, a result that gave Kay her first All-Ireland senior camogie title – and a story to tell. The Dublin team took the train to Cork but because the quality of fuel was so poor, due to the 'Emergency' as the Second World War was known in Ireland, the journey took 11 hours.

In 1943, as Dublin beat Cork again, the then 19-year-old won her second O'Duffy Cup, the All-Ireland senior camogie championship trophy, at Croke Park.

The following year, the Dublin team made it three in a row. However, a dispute between Dublin and the Camogie Association meant the county didn't play in the championships in 1945 and 1946, and Kay had to wait until 1948 to win a fourth title.

Kay herself opted out in 1949, but the first half of the next decade belonged to her and her team as Dublin won six consecutive O'Duffy Cups between 1950 and 1955. She played in England in 1951 and told the story that she was stopped at customs in Dun Laoghaire. When they unwrapped a set of delph that she had brought with her, they said she could keep the crockery but not the newspaper it was wrapped in as the News of the World was one of many publications banned in Ireland at the time.

Her on-pitch demeanour was that of grace under pressure, and it was a common sight to see male supporters lining up after matches to shake her hand. As she once told author Brendan Fullam: "I could fly along, rise the ball and strike all in the one motion."

In 1957, Kay was appointed Dublin captain. She played her last game in 1961, on the day she turned 38 and her team defeated Tipperary. She wasn't captain that day, but Betty 'Gerry' Hughes let her hold the cup as it was her last game. According to an Irish Times report, it was "a hard-fought game that provided Kathleen Mills with her fifteenth All-Ireland medal on her farewell appearance – an unequalled achievement".

In triumph, her teammates carried her around Croke Park and she was later awarded a replica of the famed O'Duffy Cup.

Kay married George Hill in 1947 and the couple established the Red Seal Handbag Company, which manufactured leather goods. Kay had a flair for business, managing staff welfare, the accounts and travelling as a sales representative at a time when few women were in the role. Later, she and her husband ran the Seventh Lock pub in Ballyfermot.

Ireland's greatest camogie player died at home on 12 August 1996, two months short of her 73rd birthday. Her legacy lives on as the All-Ireland Camogie Premier Junior Championship Cup was named in her honour. Her 15 medals can be viewed at the GAA Museum in Croke Park.

A commemorative plaque on the wall of Kay's former home at 1 Abercorn Terrace in Inchicore carries the inscription: "Lithe and graceful, a superb midfield player with neat wrist work, quick to lift and strike at full speed. She could score from any angle."

RW/CF

Colleagues Honour Camogie Star

NATIONAL ORGANISER . . . Mr. Sean O'Duffy presents Kathleen Mills with a replica of the All-Ireland Cup at a reception in the C.I.E. Club, Earl Place, to mark her retirement from camogie. Also in picture (from left) are: Miss M. Fitzgerald (Treasurer, Dublin Camogie Board), Mrs. E. Redmond (President, Central Council) and Miss N. McCarthy (Chairman, Dublin Camogie Board).

From *The Irish Press*, December, 1961

Mary J.P. (Maura) Scannell

(1924-2011)

Botanist, head of the National Herbarium and recipient of the National Botanic Gardens Medal for her 'truly remarkable contributions to Irish botany'

It is instructive to read Maura Scannell's chapter on Ireland's foremost lichens expert Matilda Knowles (1864-1933) in *Stars, Shells & Bluebells*, a book on Irish women scientists and pioneers, because many of the endeavours she praises in her fellow botanist also apply to herself.

Like Matilda Knowles, she was a respected and devoted head of the National Herbarium in Dublin, a "wise counsellor of the young", a discoverer of plants new to science and a woman whose plant collection was among the largest by any single botanist.

She was an authority whose wide knowledge helped inform the work of many others on a range of topics that extended well beyond botany into history, geography, ethnography, zoology and geology. She was also the first to use her knowledge of botany to help bring the past to life. For example, she identified the kinds of wood used in making ancient Irish harps in the National Museum of Ireland.

When a range of magnificent artefacts were excavated from

Maura Scannell illustration by Holly Christine Callaghan

The Botanic Gardens in Glasnevin. Picture courtesy of Dublin City Library and Archive

the heart of Viking-founded Dublin at Wood Quay, she helped to identify the kind of wood used in objects made centuries ago in the early-medieval period. She also revealed the importance of a 19th-century oil painting – a rare example from post-Famine Ireland – by identifying the reeds being harvested in it.

Mary J. P. Scannell was born in Cork in 1924 to building contractor Patrick Scannell and his wife Margaret. She studied Botany and Zoology at University College Cork and, in 1949, was appointed Assistant Keeper of the National History Division of the National Museum. That marked the beginning of her pioneering work exploring, studying and describing the cultural and historical relevance of plants.

She researched and published over 200 papers, produced countless catalogues and amassed thousands of plant specimens and field observations.

In 1970, she supervised the transfer of the National Herbarium from the National Museum to the Botanic Gardens in Glasnevin. Among the many items transferred to the plant archive were specimens of coffee, cocoa and rubber collected by Roger Casement in the Congo Free State. He had presented them to Matilda Knowles, a friend, when he visited the Herbarium in 1904.

The oldest plants in the repository date to the 17th century when they were donated by doctor, cleric and botanist, Revd Caleb Threlkeld (1676-1728).

As well as doing her own work, Maura Scannell went out of her way to encourage anyone who showed an interest in the plant world. She took a particular interest in young people and, from the 1960s, judged the annual Young Scientist Exhibition. She found time to follow her creative hobbies, too, which included painting, sculpting, sewing and embroidery.

In 1979, she helped fellow botanist Evelyn Booth, then aged 82, complete the *Flora of County Carlow*. Maura wrote a tribute to her friend and colleague when she died 11 years later, observing: "With her extensive knowledge and ready flow of repartee, Evelyn Booth was a delightful companion on forays. Over the years she assisted many university personnel with their studies and distribution. Any request for information received an immediate response."

There was an echo of this appreciation in the tributes paid to Maura Scannell herself when she died in 2011. "Always immaculately turned out, a fount of knowledge and a remarkable conversationalist, Maura Scannell has been a central figure in Ireland's botanical world for over 60 years," read one.

Before that, in 2008, her contribution was acknowledged when she was presented with the National Botanic Gardens medal for her "truly remarkable contributions to Irish botany".

During her acceptance speech, she encouraged botanists to record everything, even the little things: "No information should ever be overlooked."

CF

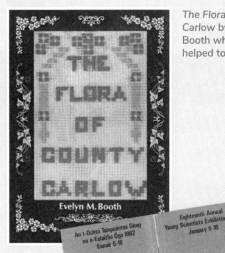

The Flora of County Carlow by Evelyn M. Booth which Maura helped to complete

'She was the first to use her knowledge of botany to help bring the past to life. She identified the kinds of wood used in making ancient Irish harps in the National Museum of Ireland'

Maura was a judge at the Young Scientist Exhibition from the 1960s

Una O'Higgins O'Malley

(1927-2005)

Peace activist, poet and founder member of the Glencree Centre for Peace and Reconciliation

Remembered by her daughter Iseult O'Malley

Una O'Higgins O'Malley, daughter of Kevin O'Higgins, Justice Minister in the fourth Dáil, was only a few months old when he was assassinated in 1927. His death and his legacy of forgiveness were the dominant influences that explain much of her public life as an adult.

She told us that, as a child, she found herself having to console total strangers who would start weeping for her father on being introduced to her. My own impression is that there were very few days in her life that she did not think of her parents.

It was the peace movement that eventually came to absorb most of Una's efforts. From the early days of protesting against the IRA outside the Sinn Féin offices, through the running of holidays in Newbridge for pensioners from Northern Ireland, to the establishment of the Glencree Centre for Peace and Reconciliation in Wicklow, there was an abiding theme to do with the necessity for the people of this island to learn to forgive and accept each other.

Along with reconciliation, an equally deep theme in Una's life

Una when she worked briefly as a solicitor for Arthur Cox

was justice. Una was involved in many organisations, and her involvement always stemmed from a feeling that injustice was happening and something should be done.

Quite apart from the peace movement, Una was involved in several projects, from helping to get Meals on Wheels going in the Mater Hospital, to trying to do something about the appalling state of housing or the conditions of Travellers in Dublin, to campaigning for the Irish Council for Civil Liberties.

She ran [unsuccessfully] as an independent in the general election of 1977, putting her in direct conflict with the party representing her family tradition, but she was convinced that the issues of reconciliation, social justice and garda misconduct required her to take a stand.

Getting Glencree established and up and running was a huge and difficult undertaking for everyone involved. There were differences over how to deal with internal issues, but the

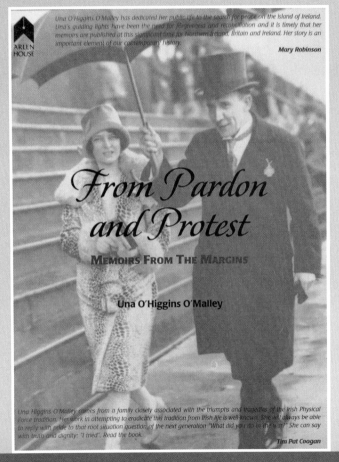

Una O'Higgins O'Malley has dedicated her public life to the search for peace on the island of Ireland. Una's guiding lights have been the need for forgiveness and reconciliation and it is timely that her memoirs are published at this significant time for Northern Ireland, Britain and Ireland. Her story is an important element of our contemporary history.

Mary Robinson

From Pardon and Protest

MEMOIRS FROM THE MARGINS

Una O'Higgins O'Malley

Una Higgins O'Malley comes from a family closely associated with the triumphs and tragedies of the Irish Physical Force tradition. Her work in attempting to eradicate this tradition from Irish life is well-known. She will always be able to reply with pride to that root situation question of the next generation 'What did you do in the war?' She can say with truth and dignity: 'I tried'. Read the book.

Tim Pat Coogan

survival of Glencree over so many decades is a tribute to those involved who learned that if you want to help others to reconcile, you must be prepared to engage in some reconciliation yourself.

Two of the most difficult moments in Una's life related to her father's legacy. The first was when, aged 60, the names of his three assassins were first published. With that publication came the story that one of the men had danced on her father's grave. That drove her temporarily into a deeply black mood. She had a Mass said for her father and the men who killed him. Her gesture was remarkable.

Later, she met with the son of one of the men involved. His account of what his father told him – that Kevin O'Higgins forgave his attackers on the roadside and said this must be the last of the killings – carries the same message of forgiveness that my mother was taught as a child.

The second deeply difficult experience was the discovery of her father's correspondence with Lady Hazel Lavery. She was very upset, but she did come to terms with the fact that her father was not perhaps as perfect as she had imagined. Una's loving commitment to her own family was absolute.

Una's favourite quotation from her father came from one of his letters: "...but we carried our brick and we laid it fair and square and as well as we knew how.."

The same can be said of her.

Una's memoir, published in 2001

Margaret MacCurtain

(1929-2020)

Feminist, pioneering historian, human-rights activist and Dominican Sister

Margaret MacCurtain. Picture courtesy of Alan Hayes

Pioneering historian Margaret MacCurtain was once compared to the Venerable Bede, the 'father of English history', and lauded for the way she had succeeded in gliding serenely over fixed ideas to open the subject up to new fields.

She challenged the master narrative to provide a compelling analysis of the historical experience of Irish women, fellow historian and champion of women Margaret Ó hÓgartaigh wrote in a glowing review of her 2008 book, *Ariadne's Thread: Writing Women into Irish History*.

Margaret MacCurtain received little support – and much resistance – when she set out to write women back into mainstream Irish history yet, she said later, her determination to do so, "had succeeded beyond her wildest dreams".

The Women's History Association of Ireland, founded with Mary Cullen, is one of her many legacies, but her work in academia was just one strand of a multi-faceted life. She was also a tireless advocate for social justice, a scholar, a reformer and a Dominican Sister.

She fought for the abolition of corporal punishment in schools and for the rights of children with special educational needs. She also campaigned against domestic violence and for the right to remarry after an annulment or civil divorce. In 1978, she joined 20,000 people on a street protest to try, unsuccessfully, to stop civic offices being built on the remains of an exceptional Viking settlement at Wood Quay in Dublin.

Margaret MacCurtain was born in 1929 in Cork into a family where banker Ann McKenna and her husband, school inspector Sean MacCurtain, put an emphasis on equality and education. All four of their daughters went to university. At University College Cork, Margaret graduated with first-class honours in English and History, winning both a gold medal and the Peel Memorial Award.

Her external examiner J.R.R. Tolkien, author of *The Lord of the Rings*, invited her to study medieval literature in Oxford with him, but she turned down the offer to enter into the Dominican order.

ARIADNE'S THREAD
Writing Women into Irish History

Margaret Mac Curtain

Margaret's 2008 book, *Ariadne's Thread, Writing Women into Irish History*

She had been open to the idea of becoming a nun from an early age and when, aged nine, she contracted diphtheria and spent months in a fever hospital without visitors, her faith deepened. "My thoughts turned to God, especially when one of my companions in that bleak ward died," she said later.

As Sr Benvenuta – Sr Ben to her students at University College Dublin (UCD) – she continued her studies, completing a first-class Master's and later PhD on the 16th-century Kerry-born bishop-diplomat Dominic O'Daly. She travelled to several European archives and became aware of the pivotal, but ignored, role played by women, setting the course for her pioneering work on women's history.

She was also a historian of early modern Ireland and her publications, including *The Birth of Modern Ireland* (1969) with Mark Tierney, and *Women in Irish Society: the Historical Dimension* (1978), a collection of essays she co-edited with Donnchadh Ó Corráin, continue to inspire generations of historians, her alma mater UCD noted in a tribute.

The university's Director of Gender Studies, Dr Mary McAuliffe, noted: "There are many, many stories of her abilities to inspire students, her kindnesses and mentorship of students, and her battles with the academic and religious institutions to which she belonged." (She was one of few members of the Catholic Church who campaigned publicly for a 'Yes' vote during the 1995 divorce referendum.)

In 1980, Margaret took time out from UCD to set up the Senior College in Ballyfermot, Dublin, so that students from disadvantaged areas would have access to education. Four of its graduates were nominated for Oscars in film animation in 2016. That happy fact was recorded in the *Irish Times* under a headline that read: "Oscars for art of the possible".

The will to pursue those possibilities, often against opposition, captures something of the essence of Margaret MacCurtain. Congregation Prioress of the Dominican Sisters, Sr Elizabeth Healy, said Margaret's courage to face difficulties and opposition head on – such as refusing to give Archbishop John Charles McQuaid her lecture notes in 1964 – were her defining characteristics.

The School of History at UCD, the university which once refused to introduce a women's history course, now awards the Margaret MacCurtain Scholarship in Women's History annually.

CF

Margaret signing copies of her book at the Dublin Festival of History in 2013. Picture courtesy of Dublin City Library and Archive

'Her external examiner J.R.R. Tolkien, author of *The Lord of the Rings*, invited her to study medieval literature in Oxford with him, but she turned down the offer to enter into the Dominican order'

In 1980, Marian Finucane became the first woman to present RTÉ's flagship programme *The Late Late Show*
Picture courtesy of Derek Speirs

Strike pickets at Dunnes Stores, Henry Street, Dublin in 1984.
Picture courtesy of RTÉ Archives

milestones

1983 The Eighth Amendment is written into the Constitution. It recognises that the unborn have an equal right to life as that of the mother.

1984 Mary Manning, a check-out worker at Dunnes Stores on Henry Street in Dublin, is suspended for following a union instruction not to handle South African grapefruit. The measure is a protest against the country's system of apartheid. Ten fellow workers go out on strike in support. The strike continues for three years, until April 1987, when South African goods are banned from Ireland.

1985 The sale of non-medical contraception without a prescription is permitted, but only in pharmacies and to those over 18.

1985 The Labour Court makes a landmark ruling in a constructive dismissal case, establishing the right to freedom from sexual harassment in the workplace (see entry on Evelyn Owens).

1990 Mary Robinson is elected the first female President of Ireland.

1994 All restrictions on contraception are removed.

1995 The constitutional ban on divorce is lifted by the slimmest of margins with 50.3% voting in favour and 49.79% against. One of the campaign's most memorable slogans is coined by Fine Gael TD Alice Glenn: "A woman voting for divorce is like a turkey voting for Christmas."

Sylvia Meehan

(1929-2018)

Pioneering chairperson of the Employment Equality Agency

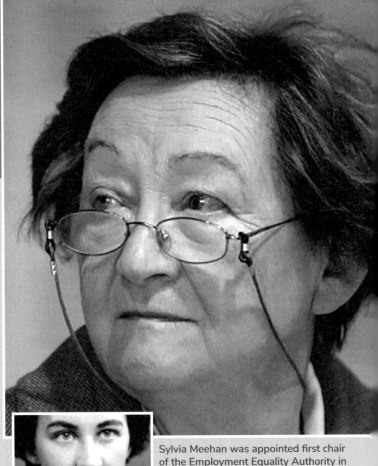

Sylvia Meehan was born Sylvia Shiel on 2 April, 1929 in Dublin. She studied legal and political science at University College Dublin (UCD), where she was the first woman to win the UCD Literary and Historical Association gold medal in 1951. When her husband Denis died in 1969, leaving her with five children under 15 to raise, she began her career in teaching at Cabinteely Community School.

She joined the Association of Secondary Teachers in Ireland (ASTI) and became very active in the union. She was elected to the Women's Committee of the Irish Congress of Trade Unions (ICTU) and was chairperson for some years. She was remembered as a determined and fearless negotiator, and as an excellent communicator who spoke throughout the 32 counties of Ireland on why equality matters.

In 1977, she was appointed as the first chair and chief executive of the Employment Equality Authority (EEA), and held that post from its establishment in 1977 until her retirement in 1992. The Authority was established to oversee the enforcement of the Employment Equality Act. Sylvia was

Sylvia Meehan was appointed first chair of the Employment Equality Authority in 1977. Picture courtesy of Derek Speirs Inset: Sylvia as a student in UCD in 1949. Picture courtesy of her family

In Sylvia's own words:

'As I was growing up, it was quite normal to pay women less for doing the same work as a man. I suppose I always knew about it. It was when I became a widow with five young children, as a newly qualified teacher, that it hit home. In a nearby school a man who was separated from his wife was paid more than me. He received a married man's allowance. There was no married woman's allowance. All over Ireland there was a male and female rate for the job, as you have just heard. The 'stronger sex', so-called, received a bulkier wage packet. I resolved to do something about that with other women in the post-1960s women's movement.

Towards the end of the 1960s, we were told that life would be wonderful if we joined the European Economic Community in 1973. You have heard, that when Ireland joined, all members states were obliged to bring in equal pay legislation. Well, that nearly did not happen here. Minister for Foreign Affairs Garret Fitzgerald asked on behalf of the then government for a derogation, for permission not to give employment equality to Irish women.

We in the women's movement were appalled. We founded the Council for the Status of Women, which exists to this day. The vast majority of Irish people agreed with us and advised the EEC to ignore the Irish government. One of our representatives on the Council for the Status of Women, the late Hilda Tweedy, went to Brussels to explain the true views of the Irish people. The government did not get its derogation and the Irish people got the right to equality in employment. That lesson taught me to put my faith in the good sense of the Irish people, in general.

Extract from Sylvia's speech on receiving the award for Professional Excellence, Griffith College 2014

universally acknowledged as being one of the most effective figures in achieving equal pay for women.

While she was in charge of the EEA, she sponsored research into problems facing girls and women in education and employment, including maternity leave and childcare. She did not confine her drive for equality to women's rights, and she argued for LGBT rights when it was not generally acceptable to do so. She also defended the rights of Travellers and immigrants to Ireland. She was a consistent contributor to pan-national meetgins and organisations as she regarded progress in equality as a universal need that transcended local politics.

In 1997, the University of Limerick conferred Sylvia with an honorary Doctorate of Laws, in recognition of her contribution to making Irish society a better place for all.

Following her retirement from the EEA, she served as President

Campaigning for equal rights and equal pay for women, Sligo 1983. Picture courtesy of Derek Speirs

of the Irish Senior Citizens Parliament, leading campaigns against ageism and for inclusion of older people in all aspects of society. She was also a board member of the Age and Opportunity (A&O) organisation for older people. Mary Robinson, former President of Ireland, presented Sylvia with the 'People of the Year' award for giving a voice to those who might otherwise be forgotten, and for her skill and tenacity in asserting the rights of older people.

Sylvia never stopped campaigning and came to the fore yet again in 2008 when she led A&O's campaign against the abolition of the universal entitlement to the medical card for the over-70s. Speaking at a protest outside Leinster House, which saw 20,000 older people gathered on the streets, she said: "Older people have become more confident and I am thrilled that this confidence is expressing itself."

Until its absorption into the Department of Health in 2009, Sylvia was also an active member of the National Council on Ageing and Older People.

The President, Michael D. Higgins, said her pioneering work on equality in education and employment had left a lasting legacy: "In her life, Sylvia Meehan overcame many challenges, becoming a tenacious campaigner for workers' rights, determined to promote the inclusion and empowerment of women, older people, and all vulnerable sections of society... Her energy, vision and dynamism were directed at making Ireland a more empowering, informed, and welcoming society."

MM

Sylvia's daughter Rosa Meehan recalls:

'My own memories are of going to Wexford with her as a child, and how she would love to talk to the farming women she became friends with there, ditto on our many visits to cousins in Carlow, She had spent many summers as a child in Carlow. She was always interested in people's lives and to my eyes as a child seemed comfortable with everybody.'

Evelyn Owens

(1931-2010)

Trade unionist and women's rights activist who successfully fought against pay discrimination

Evelyn Owens was a woman who had many 'firsts' in her remarkable life. She was the first female President of the Irish Local Government Officials Union (ILGOU); the first female Chairperson of the Labour Court; the first female leas-Cathaoirleach of the Seanad and the first woman to sign a piece of legislation into Irish law.

She was born in Vernon Gardens, Clontarf, Dublin, close to the Holy Faith Convent school where she was educated. She was a good student who achieved high marks in the public examinations. In 1948, she passed the Dublin Corporation entrance examinations and started work as a clerical officer in the City Treasurer's department. Later, she studied part-time for a diploma in public administration in Trinity College Dublin.

Evelyn joined the ILGOU, where she became a very effective activist. In 1963, rather than accept the union's recommendation on a controversial pay deal, she organised a meeting of 94 women, who established the Association of Women Officers of the Local Authorities of Ireland (AWOLAO).

Evelyn Owens. All pictures courtesy of Fórsa trade union

Evelyn was voted into the chair and soon the membership of the new association had risen to 146.

The women mounted a legal challenge to the ILGOU and secured an injunction to prevent the union accepting the deal. They lobbied the union, local authorities and, eventually, the Dáil. The male rate was applied to all clerical workers, together with the 12 per cent award from the national pay agreement – a resounding victory for the women.

A politicised Evelyn emerged as a radicalising influence within the ILGOU. Her efforts impressed ILGOU members, who elected her their vice-president (1964-7) and president (1967-9), making her the first woman president of an Irish union representing both sexes.

She was also active within the wider trade union movement as a member of the Irish Congress of Trade Unions' (ICTU) women's advisory council, serving as its chairwoman from 1968 to 1971.

Evelyn was elected to Seanad Éireann in 1969 on the Labour Panel, and used this platform to press for equality of pay and employment opportunities for women, co-education in schools, and the rights

of abandoned wives, distressed widows, and single mothers. She was also a member of the Council for the Status of Women in the early 1970s, and chair of the Labour Party's women's national council from 1975.

Upon re-election to the Seanad in 1973, she was appointed the first female leas-Cathaoirleach (deputy chairperson). As a member of the presidential commission, she became the first woman to sign an Irish bill into law in 1974. In early 1976, Evelyn was prominent in protests when the Government tried unsuccessfully to postpone implementing its equal pay legislation.

Just before the Government left office in 1977, she pushed legislation through the Seanad outlawing employment discrimination on the grounds of sex and marital status. However, she lost her seat at the next election.

Evelyn was appointed to the Labour Court in 1984 and her influence was soon apparent. The court made a landmark ruling in a 1985 constructive dismissal case, which established the right to freedom from sexual harassment in the workplace.

Much of the case law subsequently developed by the Labour Court regarding gender discrimination and sexual harassment was incorporated into equality legislation passed by the Oireachtas in 1998. Evelyn was promoted to chairwoman of the Labour Court in 1994.

She chaired the National Minimum Wage Commission (1997-8), paving the way for the introduction of a minimum wage in 2001. After retiring from the Labour Court in 1998, she became an honorary member of the boards of Beaumont Hospital and the Irish Medical Council. She died on 26 September 2010.

MM

'Just before the Government left office in 1977, Evelyn pushed legislation through the Seanad outlawing employment discrimination on the grounds of sex and marital status'

Evelyn Owens. All pictures courtesy of Fórsa trade union

Pat Crowley

(1933-2013)

Fashion designer

"You just had to have a Pat Crowley in your wardrobe," said Cecily McMenamin, former fashion director for Brown Thomas, speaking about the designer who, for three decades, dressed some of the most stylish women in Ireland and abroad.

Her clients included Miranda Guinness, countess of Iveagh, and Eileen, Lady Mount Charles. President Mary Robinson wore Pat Crowley designs for such significant occasions as her visit to the Vatican and her meeting with Queen Elizabeth in London.

Miranda Guinness said: "Pat had an amazing imagination and she was very inventive. I think she was almost psychic. She dressed me regularly and I always felt frightfully happy in her clothes. She dressed you in such a witty way, to fit your character. And she herself was terribly stylish."

Patricia Crowley was born on 17 May, 1933, in Taylor's Hill, Galway, the eldest child of Hubert Vernon, who worked for the Bank of Ireland, and Margaret, who was from a prosperous family of grain and seed merchants from Cork.

'Pat had an amazing imagination and she was very inventive. I think she was almost psychic'
- Miranda Guinness

After school, Pat studied fashion at the newly opened Grafton Academy of Dress Design in Dublin. Her motivation was simple. "My mother said that a girl should always know how to make her own clothes."

Next up was a stint as an air hostess with Aer Lingus, a job considered so glamorous at the time it might be compared to that of a film star or celebrity today. She got the opportunity to see the world and she was even a member of the crew on the first transatlantic flight from Ireland.

She met her husband-to-be during a Lansdowne Road rugby international. Conor Crowley of the accountancy firm Stokes Kennedy Crowley was there with his mother. When she suggested that he ask Pat out, he revealed that he already had, according to an anecdote from the *Sunday Independent*. A lifelong love match was made.

After their wedding, Pat gave up her job in Aer Lingus as women were obliged, under the marriage bar, to leave public service jobs. But she had no intention of giving up her career and instead went to work for renowned designer Irene Gilbert in her Dublin atelier.

Working with Irene played a key role in shaping Pat's future career. She perfected her technical skills and also learned how to understand the needs of prospective clients.

1968 was a momentous year for her – her first child Vernon was born and she launched her own business, designing cutting-edge knitwear inspired by Irish traditions. She would employ over 600 hand-knitters at one stage. In the 1970s she introduced a couture line, which was sold in her shop on Duke Street in Dublin. She also stocked European designers such as Valentino, Ungaro and Thierry Mugler.

American customers loved her designs and she was quoted in a US newspaper as saying "even though we are in the middle of a financial recession, there is no need to suffer a personal depression by denying ourselves beautiful clothes".

As well as Vernon, Pat and Conor had two daughters, Lisa and Fiona. The children grew up at Carpenterstown in Dublin. Pat, a keen horsewoman, rode daily.

In 1999, just a few months after she broke her hip, Pat's husband Conor died suddenly. Not long after this bereavement, she was diagnosed with Alzheimer's disease and she died aged 80.

She was a trailblazer in Irish fashion whose innate style and elegance was her calling card.

RW

All pictures courtesy of
Pat Crowley's family

Prof Barbara Wright

(1935-2019)

Pioneering academic, scholar and one of the first female fellows of TCD

Remembered by former student and colleague Dr Derval Conroy

When 8 March was chosen as International Women's Day in 1977, Barbara Wright must have allowed herself a smile. Born on 8 March herself, daughter of one of the early women medical graduates in Ireland, Rosaleen Hoskin, and destined for a brilliant academic career in French Studies, the ideals underpinning International Women's Day were close to her heart.

Following the award of her PhD at Cambridge University in 1962, Barbara returned to her undergraduate alma mater, Trinity College Dublin, where she played a key role in the promotion of French Studies in Ireland until her retirement in 2005, and beyond. In her many roles as professor, as Dean of Arts (Letters), as a senior fellow, she fostered careers, established new degree programmes, built networks with French institutions, always with a rigorous commitment to academic standards.

Her own research interests focused largely on 19th-century French literature and painting, and the relationship

Prof Barbara Wright was born on 8 March, which later became International Women's Day. Picture courtesy of her son Jonathan Wright

Barbara receiving the title *Chevalier de l'Ordre National du Mérite*

the type of project that today would only be undertaken by a team, armed with considerable technical resources.

Of particular Irish interest is her edition in 2012 of the diaries of the Celtic art specialist and archaeologist Françoise Henry (herself one of the first women elected to the Royal Irish Academy in 1949), under the title *Les Îles d'Inishkea: carnets personnels.*

An ardent music-lover, Barbara was an accomplished pianist and influential member of the governing body of the Royal Irish Academy of Music. Over the years, she was awarded numerous accolades and honours, from being one of the first four women to be elected to a Fellowship in Trinity in 1968 to being awarded, most exceptionally, the title of the French *Chevalier de la Légion d'honneur* in 2019.

Faced with a terminal illness, Barbara lived her final months with the generosity and dignity and drive that characterised her career. Those few months were busy, she mentioned at the time; there was a lot to do. One of her projects was the publication of the 19th-century account by Édouard de Tocqueville of his travels

between them. Some of her most pioneering work, which remains unsurpassed, focuses on French writer and painter Eugène Fromentin, including the publication in 1995 of his correspondence in two volumes, totalling over 2,400 pages –

around England, Scotland and Ireland, seen through subsequently to fruition by friends and colleagues.

Fromentin's home town of La Rochelle has long acknowledged Barbara's work concerning their native son, not least by making her a honorary citizen some years ago. This summer, that recognition takes a leap further, and embeds her legacy very concretely in the fabric of the city in the naming of a walkway after her, the *allée* Barbara Wright. While those who take that *allée* might wonder who this Irish woman was, many others will know. Barbara was the person who saw possibilities, opportunities, potential, who made introductions and opened doors, who made things happen.

At the memorable *Légion d'honneur* ceremony in the French ambassador's residence in Ailesbury Road, shortly before she died, everyone in the room had a story of a gesture, great or small, of support and encouragement: an invitation to the Concert Hall for a young colleague newly-arrived; to lunch in Trinity's Common Room for a returning early career researcher; encouragement at a book launch; enthusiasm for an exhibition; praise for a project; or simply a funny anecdote, testament to Barbara's dry sense of humour.

So while for some, the Tocqueville volume, dedicated to her grandchildren Max and Lexi, is her final gift to the international community of French scholars, for others that gift lies elsewhere.

'Barbara was the person who saw possibilities, opportunities, potential, who made introductions and opened doors, who made things happen'

Barbara receiving the title *Chevalier de la Légion d'honneur*

Monica Barnes

(1936-2018)

Politician, women's rights activist and co-founder of the Council for the Status of Women

Remembered by her daughter Sarah Barnes

One of my earliest memories is hearing the clickety-clack of my mother's typewriter. My mother would type, sitting at the large oak table in the kitchen, smoke floating up from her cigarette in the ashtray, with a mug of strong coffee at her side. It was before the invention of the photocopier and we had the copying technology of the day, a Roneo Stencil machine. My father would run off whatever my mother had typed up, usually a speech or press release.

After rush hour, we would drive to Dublin city, where the newspapers were based, and either myself, or my siblings would jump out of the car, run to the newspaper office, with an envelope containing the speech, marked "For Immediate Release".

My mother was a committed feminist and liberal all her life. She was greatly influenced by her father, a committed trade unionist who worked in the Gypsum Industries Factory in their hometown of Kingscourt, Co Cavan.

She won a county council scholarship to the St Louis Convent in Carrickmacross, Co Monaghan, as a boarder. Her ambition was to become a teacher.

However, during her Leaving Certificate Maths exam she "went blank", which meant she couldn't progress to third level. Instead, she went to Belfast and did a course in journalism and business studies. She spent a few years working in London, including as a clerk in the London Stock Exchange. She met my father, Bob, shortly after returning to Ireland in 1960 and they married in 1962.

Initially they lived in a flat in Rathmines in Dublin and myself, my brother and sister were all born within four years. At that time, she felt very isolated and suffered from post-natal depression, although it was not recognised as that at the time. Instead, a doctor told her to "pull herself together".

In her speeches of the 1970s she relentlessly highlighted the dire situation and position of women in Irish society. Early 1973, saw the publication of the Report of the Commission on the Status of Women. It identified 49 discriminations to be removed and 19 suggestions as to how the status of women in Ireland could be improved. That year also saw the removal of the marriage bar, where women in the public service and most other employment were forced to give up their careers and economic independence upon marriage.

1973 was also the year Ireland joined what was then called the

EEC. As a member state, Ireland had to implement European legislation into Irish law, which were significant steps forward for Irish women; the Equal Pay Act was introduced in 1974, followed by the Employment Equality Act (1977), which also set up the Employment Equality Agency. The then Minister for Labour, Michael O'Leary, appointed my mother as one of the members of the Agency. She also co-founded the Council for the Status of Women in 1973.

She believed fighting for reforms from outside the political system would never be as effective as fighting for change from inside the system. In 1975, she founded and was chairwoman of Women Elect, an organisation that encouraged and supported women to stand for election. Many women TDs and ministers began their political careers in Women Elect.

Elected to the Seanad in early 1982, my mother was elected to the Dáil in November 1982. In 1983, she trenchantly opposed the wording of the Eighth Amendment to the Constitution – which recognised the equal right to life of the pregnant woman and the unborn – and was one of only two women TDs to vote against it (Eileen Desmond of Labour was the other). She later recalled how she was subjected to a campaign of hate mail and death threats during that period.

In an interview in the *Sunday Independent* shortly before she died, she said: "I remember saying to Gemma [Hussey] that I did not get elected to the Dáil after all these years of working for women to sell them out. For me, I had to stand up for women, and for the health and future of women."

All pictures courtesy of Monica's daughter
Sarah Barnes

Eilís Mullan

(1936-2004)

Artistic director of Dublin Youth Theatre and inspirational force in youth drama

What do Game of *Thrones*, *Fair City* and the *Barabbas* Theatre Company have in common? They all involve people who were mentored by Eilís Mullan, the former artistic director of Dublin Youth Theatre (DYT).

A legendary figure within the Irish acting world, she was renowned for her encouragement of young people and her unwavering interest in their ideas.

Actor Peter Hanly, who starred in *Braveheart* and *Ballykissangel*, remembers being "a very green teenager" entering Dublin Youth Theatre long ago: "She continually bolstered my self-confidence – every workshop, rehearsal, performance, every little exchange I had with Eilís made me feel better about myself."

She was also persuasive, as Peter adds: "It was hard to say no to Eilís and indeed why would you want to"?

Eilís was born in 1936 and lived in Rathgar, Dublin. She was the eldest in a family of three girls and three boys. She attended University College Dublin as a mature student

From *The Crucible* in 1987.
Picture courtesy of Youth Theatre Ireland

studying English and economics. She was working at the Department of Agriculture when she became involved with youth theatre, initially on a voluntary basis. Then, her friend and the founder of DYT, Paddy O'Dwyer, asked her to become its artistic director. She never looked back.

In the early 1990s, she took on the full-time role of director of the National Association of Youth Drama (NAYD), which was based in Gardiner Street in Dublin.

From *A Midsummer Night's Dream* in 1985. Picture courtesy of Youth Theatre Ireland

She was determined to give as many young people as possible access to the theatre. When she was first involved with NAYD, there were fewer than 20 youth theatre groups in the country. By the time she retired in 2003, the number had tripled to 74.

She knew from her very first directing job that she had discovered her life's work. She said she loved the honesty and enthusiasm of youth.

"Working with young people on a show is an experience, every single time," she said. "They might drive you mad, miss the odd rehearsal and all that, but in the end, they always pull out all the stops. You come up with an idea, they give it 150 per cent."

Though, she explained that it was difficult, too, because you had to take on young people's problems: "Adults have different compartments for things but they don't, and you can't abandon them at the end of the workshop."

Many well-known stars of Irish stage and screen enjoyed support from Eilís at the start of their career. Her charges

> '**She continually bolstered my self-confidence –
> every workshop, rehearsal, performance, every
> little exchange I had with Eilís made me feel better
> about myself**' – Actor Peter Hanly

included Aidan Gillen, Jasmine Russell, Fionnuala Murphy, Veronica Coburn, David Parnell, and Clelia Murphy among many others.

For Philip McMahon of THISISPOPBABY theatre company, Eilís changed the face of youth arts in Ireland.

Innovative and unafraid to take a risk, Eilís commissioned and produced new work for youth theatres by Peter Sheridan and Antoine Ó Flatharta. She directed Gerard Stembridge's first play and she organised NAYD's young playwright competition, which shone a light on playwright and screenwriter Mark O'Rowe for the first time.

Eilís also loved James Joyce and Shakespeare. She was President of the Dublin Shakespeare Society, directing plays including *King Lear*, *Macbeth* and *Twelfth Night* as well as a production of *Rosencrantz and Guildenstern Are Dead* featuring Gabriel Byrne and Myles Dungan.

Eilís lived in Portobello for the last 15 years of her life, a home she shared with her eldest niece, Ruth. Although she was ill, she came out of hospital on polling day in June 2004 to cast her vote. She died less than two weeks later.

From *Ask Too Much of Me*, a 2019 Youth Theatre Ireland production. Picture courtesy of Ros Kavanagh

Eoghan Doyle of Youth Theatre Ireland (formerly NAYD) says Eilís Mullan is directly responsible for the organisation that Youth Theatre Ireland is today. "Her belief in young people and the power of youth theatre has enabled Youth Theatre Ireland to continue to support over 2,000 young people right across Ireland to access youth theatres within their communities. She placed the voice of young people at the centre of the work of the organisation."

RW

Mavis Arnold

(1937-2017)

Women's rights activist, psychotherapist and investigative journalist who exposed widespread abuse in church-run Industrial Schools

In the early 1970s, Mavis Arnold chanced across Heather Laskey, a freelance journalist she knew slightly when she had been a student. For a reason Heather can't explain, she asked Mavis for help: "I want to write a book about an orphanage in Cavan."

"So do I," replied Mavis.

Heather recalls the meeting, explaining that the idea of the book was prompted by her psychiatrist husband Jim O'Brien. He had urged her to look into the Industrial School known as St Joseph's Orphanage after hearing from a patient about the appalling abuse she and other children had suffered at the hands of the Poor Clare nuns who ran it.

At the time, Mavis had given refuge in her home in Dublin to an unmarried pregnant woman who had spent her childhood at the same institution. Over a number of months, the young woman had opened up and spoke, with "her shoulders hunched, rocking", of the years of maltreatment she had experienced before being thrown out into the world, utterly ignorant, at 16.

Mavis Arnold. Picture courtesy of Derek Speirs

‘When her phone was tapped in the 1980s, Mavis joked that the only thing anyone listening in would have heard was "earfuls of talk" about the women's movement’

Mavis outside the High Court with her husband Bruce Arnold and fellow journalist Geraldine Kennedy who challenged the improper tapping of their telephones in 1982. Picture courtesy of Derek Speirs

The two journalists collected similar testimony from other survivors going back decades: of fighting for left-over food from the hens' bucket, of arbitrary violence, and neglect of healthcare and education. They also investigated and told the terrible story of the tragic fire that had taken the lives of 35 children in 1943.

Together, with their wider research into the operation of Ireland's vast Industrial School system, they put their catalogue of Church and State abuse and illegalities into a groundbreaking book, *Children of the Poor Clares*. After six years trying to find a publisher, it was eventually published by Appletree Press in Belfast in 1985.

The book was initially greeted with disbelief and sceptical reviews. But more and more, other exposés relating to physical and sexual abuses in similar Church-run institutions became public knowledge, eventually leading to a State apology and a government investigation into Church-run Industrial and Reform schools. The Commission to Enquire into Child Abuse, or the Ryan Commission as it was known, reported in 2009, confirming the scandalous hidden reality of Church care for the children first revealed by Mavis Arnold and Heather Laskey.

Ysabel Mavis Cleave was born in 1937 in India to Mayor John Cleave and his wife Mary. As a child, she and her mother and sister Maureen were rescued when their ship, travelling from India, was torpedoed by the Germans during the Second World War. Her father was not with them on that occasion.

Mavis spent her childhood in Sligo and later studied in

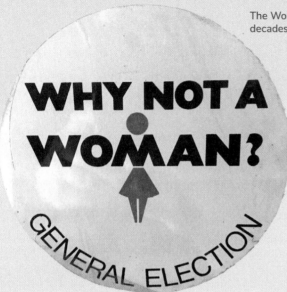

(WPA) with former minister Gemma Hussey, Hilary Pratt, Dr Mary Henry and Audrey Conlon, to encourage more women to run for election.

'Why not a woman?' ran its catchy slogan.

Audrey Conlon remembers Mavis as a woman who was great company, witty and self-deprecating. She was also a magnificent cook, she says, and once played host to American feminist Betty Friedan who spoke at one of the Women's Political Association's seminars: "It was a riot of an evening," recalls Audrey, explaining that she had bumped into Betty Friedan in a lift at a conference in Denmark and invited her to Ireland.

In the 1980s, Mavis and Bruce Arnold's home phone was tapped because her husband was thought to pose a possible threat to national security. Mavis later joked that the only thing anyone listening in would have heard was "earfuls of talk" about the women's movement.

She remained active and involved until she got Alzheimer's disease in her 70s, but even then, she continued to walk with the B Team walking group. The members, many of them colleagues at the Women's Political Association, sang to her to keep her going when her energy flagged.

When she died in 2017, her husband Bruce Arnold said that she was always on the side of the oppressed and disenfranchised. "Her life story lives on after her," he said.

CF

Alexandra College in Dublin and Trinity College where she met her future husband, journalist Bruce Arnold. They married in 1959 and endured the loss of their first daughter Emma who died in 1961. The couple had three more children, Hugo, Samuel and Polly.

While Mavis saw her role primary as a home-maker – she was an outstanding cook and baker – she also became politically active. In 1969, she founded the Women's Political Association

Deirdre Kelly

(1938-2001)

A conservationist focused on the future

Once described as "the conscience of the city", Dubliner Deirdre Kelly was a woman far head of her time. A conservationist and an environmental campaigner, she was involved in the Wood Quay marches against the building of civic offices on Viking settlements in the capital in the late 1970s.

She took part in the protests over the demolition of Georgian buildings off St Stephen's Green, which became known as the Battle for Hume Street. As well as wanting to preserve our past, she also wanted a future for Dublin in which the heart of the city was thriving.

The former Professor of History, Kevin B. Nowlan, who worked with Deirdre in the Dublin Civic Group, described her as someone who had "a great awareness all the time that a city is about the people who live in it and not just buildings".

Deirdre was born on 15 May 1938 in Dublin, the eldest daughter of Thomas and Mary McMahon's four children. She was educated locally at Scoil Bhríde in Ranelagh followed

Deirdre Kelly. Picture courtesy
of The O'Brien Press

DEIRDRE KELLY

Four Roads to Dublin
THE HISTORY OF
Ranelagh, Rathmines and Leeson Street

Picture courtesy of The O'Brien Press

Above right: from the *Irish Press* in 1976

Launching their book, "Hands Off Dublin", author Deirdre Kelly and photographer Pat Langan point out the spot at Ballybough where a motorway is planned to run along the Royal Canal. At the rear, a spur of the motorway would cut through the sportsfields at Croke Park. The terrace of houses on the right would also be demolished.

by Holy Faith Convent in Haddington Road. After she studied at the College of Commerce in Rathmines and at the National College of Art, she worked as an archaeological artist doing pen-and-ink drawings of objects at the National Museum of Ireland. She later studied history and archaeology at University College Dublin.

She met future husband Aidan Kelly, who was attending the School of Architecture in Bolton Street, in McDaid's pub off Grafton Street. When she completed her BA in 1970, the two married and spent three months travelling through Europe.

On their return to Dublin, the couple made their home in a basement flat on Fitzwilliam St. Her years living in the historical core of the capital's south city area had a profound effect on her. She was viscerally opposed to the wave of so-called progress that involved the replacement of historic buildings with brutalist statement architecture.

'The conservationist and environmental campaigner was once described as "the conscience of the city"'

She took part in the six-month sit-in during the Battle of Hume St. The protesters objected to plans by Green Property Company to replace Georgian buildings with office

212

development. In June 1970, the protest was dispersed at the direction of the builders.

When Deirdre founded the Living City Group (LCG) in the early 1970s, her aim was to transform central Dublin into "the living heart of a capital city". She made a striking visual illustration of her point in her book *Hands Off Dublin*, published by The O'Brien Press in 1976. This addressed the detrimental impact of road planning policy on the capital.

At first, Deirdre ran the LCG from her flat but, after she had four children – Maeve, Diarmuid, Mahon and Hughie – the family, and the LCG with it, moved to Old Mount Pleasant in Ranelagh.

In 1986, she helped organise the Dublin Crisis Conference. This was a gathering of 100 groups who shared a common concern for the future of the city, ranging from environmentalists to civil rights campaigners. By 2000, Dublin Corporation had established a partnership with the Dublin Civic Trust 'Historic heart of Dublin' project, which was funded by the EU. Number 9 Merchant's Quay, which was completely derelict, was bought in 1997 and underwent an extraordinary transformation.

She also wrote *Four Roads to Dublin*, a history of Ranelagh,

A protest by architectural students at the proposed demolition of Georgian houses by a property developer on Hume Street, Dublin in 1969. Picture courtesy of RTÉ Archives

Rathmines and Leeson Street, which was published in 1995. When she died five years later, aged 61, her publisher Michael O'Brien said Deirdre would have been "pleased that people had moved back into the city and that areas had been pedestrianised. She would have felt that some of her battles paid off".

RW

Maeve Binchy

(1939-2012)

Novelist, journalist, editor, columnist and speaker

Remembered by her niece Sarah Binchy

It was in Stephen's Green in Dublin that Maeve Binchy, then a First Arts student at University College Dublin in nearby Earlsfort Terrace, had a revelation. "I was sitting on a bench in my old school coat. I looked awful and childish. I was thinking, 'Gosh, if only I had a navy duffel coat I wouldn't look so ludicrous, and the boys would fancy me'."

She put down her book and watched the people all around her. Suddenly it was as clear as daylight. "Nobody is looking at me. It doesn't matter what I'm wearing. All these people walking through Stephen's Green are wondering how they look."

It was, she said, a liberation. From that day, she embraced college life. Shedding her self-consciousness opened other doors: to travelling alone, far and wide, in the long summer holidays after she'd qualified as a teacher; to writing with ease, without fretting about the impression she was making. "I thought, if I can talk, I can write."

A chatty letter home from a kibbutz in Israel delighted her parents so much that they sent it to a newspaper as a travel

Maeve Binchy. Picture courtesy of RTÉ Archives

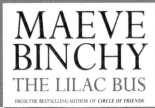

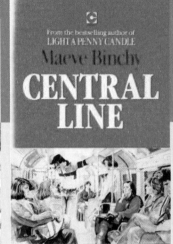

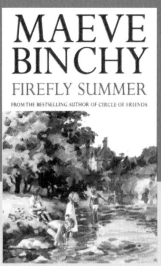

Original cover artwork from some of Maeve's many bestsellers

feature: her career as a journalist had begun.

Maeve Binchy was born to William and Maureen Binchy, a barrister and nurse, parents "who thought all their geese were swans". The eldest of four, she grew up in Dalkey. After her BA in French and History, she taught in girls' schools, freelancing on the side, until she joined the Irish Times in 1968 as women's editor.

From her earliest journalism, her voice is unmistakable: funny, intimate, observant, humane, gently impatient with all the silly social rules and conventions and imprisoning mindsets that can stunt people's lives.

In the early 1970s, having met the BBC broadcaster Gordon Snell, she moved to London as the *Irish Times* London correspondent; she and Gordon married in 1977. With his encouragement, she started writing short stories and plays. But it was her novel *Light A Penny Candle*, published in 1982, an epic tale of the friendship of two girls, one Irish, one English, which brought her fame and fortune.

'Among her fans were Oprah Winfrey, Tom Hanks and Barbara Bush; among her honours, she was particularly proud of the PEN award for lifetime achievement, presented to her in 2007 by Declan Kiberd.'

The paperback rights sold at auction for a record-breaking £52,000; the book found readers all over the world. Women's fiction at that time was dominated by romance and fantasy, but here was a book in which the female characters didn't get swept off their feet, but figured out life for themselves, in all its messiness and complexity.

By the 1990s, Maeve and Gordon were living full-time in Dalkey. With iron discipline, they got up early each morning to write side-by-side in their upstairs study. They also made plenty of time for family and friends, for socialising and fun. Maeve wrote more than 20 books at that desk, with translations into 37 languages, many film adaptations and sales of over 40 million. Among her fans were Oprah Winfrey, Tom Hanks and Barbara Bush; among her honours, she was particularly proud of the PEN award for lifetime achievement, presented to her in 2007 by Declan Kiberd.

She's remembered with deep affection in her home city. A vibrant new generation of Irish writers, encouraged and inspired by her, pay tribute at the annual *Echoes* festival in Dalkey, and she's celebrated alongside Joyce at the Museum of Literature Ireland on Stephen's Green – just yards away from the park bench of her own student epiphany.

And her readers are everywhere. People who may never have met her but who treasure her for the books that have provided them with such pleasure and good company, the whole of their lives.

Deirdre O'Connell

(1939-2001)

Actor, folk singer, director, teacher and founder of the Focus Theatre

There are many words to describe the talents and many endeavours of Eleanor Deirdre O'Connell, the woman who founded the Focus Theatre in Dublin in 1967, but it is in talking to the people she touched during her lifetime that a picture of the real woman emerges.

Phyl Herbert, for instance, went on to be a theatre director after studying at the Focus in its first year. She recalls Deirdre O'Connell as a woman of deep compassion who was responsible for introducing the Stanislavski system of acting to Ireland.

"Nobody had heard about improvisation before," she says. "It was like gaining a second skin to go through her studio training sessions. The life of any character was stripped back, analysing the background of the circumstances of the life in order to delve deeply into the script life."

She remembers Deirdre's presence too: "She always wore black, and her blue eyes sparkled beneath a crown of reddish-blonde hair draped on her head in a chignon".

Deirdre O'Connell. Picture from the Finnegan Collection, courtesy of Dublin City Library and Archive

Eleanor Deirdre O'Connell, as she was christened, might have taken a completely different path. She was born to Irish nationalist parents – Michael Joe O'Connell from Sligo and Nellie Taafe from Cork – in the Bronx, New York, in 1939.

From an early age, she showed a talent for acting and her parents encouraged it. After school, she won a scholarship for night classes at Erwin Piscator's New York Dramatic Workshop and moved into a flat with Jane Fonda and Barbra Streisand.

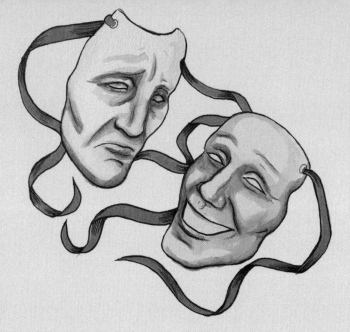

bought the Focus Theatre with financial help from her husband, singer Luke Kelly of the Dubliners. The couple had married in 1965.

The 65-seat theatre opened in 1967. Initially, plays were not well-attended, but its pioneering work soon won critical acclaim and a following. It went on to shape one of the most important chapters in Ireland's theatre history.

In the little coffee room backstage, the walls told the story of the people who paved the way. Photographs of actors – such as Mary Elizabeth Burke Kennedy, Tim McDonnell, Tom Hickey, Gabriel Byrne, Joan Bergin, Sabina Coyne (now Sabina Higgins and wife of President Michael D. Higgins) – hung on the wall, with a Brian Bourke portrait of Deirdre herself taking pride of place.

She won acclaim for her roles in Arthur Miller and Tennessee Williams plays on Broadway, and was later invited by director Lee Strasberg to join the prestigious Actor's Studio (Marlon Brando and Marilyn Monroe were graduates). She was introduced to the Stanislavski system of acting there.

Her sights, however, had been set on Ireland since her first visit aged 17. She returned in 1963 and used Ursula White-Lennon's Pocket Theatre on Ely Place in Dublin to establish the first Stanislavski Studio. When it was sold, she raised funds by singing – she was a noted folk singer – in London and

Tim McDonnell recalls: "Deirdre was so much more than our acting teacher, she was our educator in all aspects of the arts. She moulded us, taught us about music, art, literature. She showed us how to reach deep inside to the actor within, to find our truth."

When Tim was injured in a shooting accident in New York, Deirdre called him every day. When he found out he would not walk again, she would not listen to his fears that his acting life was over. "Deirdre would have none of it. She said 'ten legs or no legs, you will always have a place here at the Focus'."

In its five-decade history, the Focus Theatre staged more than 250 productions and introduced the classics, such as Chekhov, Ibsen and Strindberg, to Irish audiences. Looking back, Deirdre O'Connell later said: "It [teaching] is the deepest form of human communication that I know I have to give... It is an act of love."

That act of love resonates still. Actor Gay Murphy says Deirdre "was an inspiration, a mentor and a nurturer of talent". She studied at Focus in 1979 along with Donal O'Kelly, Bairbre Ní Chaoimh, Joan Sheehy, Bernie Downes, Sean Campion and Eamonn Hunt, and says those lucky enough to have been part of her studio would agree that she changed their lives.

Former student Robert Coyle echoes that sentiment: "Deirdre was a lifelong friend, inspirational actor, and extraordinary teacher. She is missed in so many ways."

CF

Deirdre O'Connell, left, and Joan Morrissey in *The Advertisement* by Natalia Ginsberg at the Focus Theatre, Dublin, 1976. Picture from the Finnegan Collection, courtesy of Dublin City Library and Archive

A mural tribute to Savita Halappanavar in Dublin.
Picture courtesy of Derek Speirs

Ireland votes to repeal the Eighth amendment of the Constitution.
Picture courtesy of the Sunday Independent

milestones

The last Magdalene laundry closes on Sean McDermott Street in Dublin.	**1996**
Dentist Savita Halappanavar dies from sepsis at Galway University Hospital after her request for an abortion is denied on legal grounds. Her death reignites the campaign to change Ireland's abortion laws.	**2012**
Local historian Catherine Corless uncovers evidence that 796 babies were buried in a sewage tank in a former mother and baby institution run by the Bon Secours Sisters in Tuam, Co Galway. The story makes headlines all around the world.	**2014**
Ireland votes by 66.4% to 33.6% to repeal the Eighth Amendment of the Constitution, to allow for the regulation of the termination of pregnancy through legislation.	**2018**
The final report of the Mother and Baby Homes Commission of Investigation finds that 9,000 babies died in Church-run institutions for unmarried women between 1922 and 1998. There is widespread controversy over the Commission's decision to delete the testimony of over 500 survivors. The testimony is eventually retrieved, although survivors continue to say their concerns were not heard.	**2021**
Minister for Justice Helen McEntee is the first female minister to have a baby while in office. A special accommodation had to be found to allow her to retain her position and take time off after her baby was born, as there wasn't (and still isn't) any provision for maternity leave for elected public representatives.	**2021**

Nan Joyce

(1940-2018)

Traveller rights campaigner and the first person from that community to stand in a general election

Traveller rights activist Nan Joyce famously gave an impromptu speech at the 10th anniversary seminar of Trócaire, the Catholic overseas development agency, in 1983 that got more attention, and applause, than any of the other reports and speeches.

In it, she urged Irish bishops to address the plight of the Travellers at home, who suffered as many diseases as the children of the Third World.

"You people are very concerned about the Third World," she said. "I think you should also be concerned about us; we are the Fourth World. We live among rats in camps or caravans... We may have a bit more food but we are treated in the same way as the unfortunate people of the dèveloping countries."

She later described how she had "crashed" the event – "I'm always crashing places I'm not wanted" – and saw a few red faces among the 350 attendees representing 22 countries.

By then, Nan Joyce had already made history when she became the first Traveller to stand in a general election. She

Nan Joyce. Picture courtesy of Derek Speirs

A young Traveller girl outside her makeshift home at Cherry Orchard, near Ballyfermot in Dublin in 1968. Nan Joyce highlighted the squalid conditions Travellers were forced to live in. Picture courtesy of RTÉ Archives

Nan on a Travellers' protest march in Dublin in July 1982, to demand justice and rights for Travellers.
Photo courtesy of Derek Speirs

stood as an Independent candidate in Dublin South-West in 1982 and campaigned solely on the issue of Traveller rights.

Ann Joyce, Traveller, mother of 11 children, grandmother and Irish citizen, as she described herself on her election manifesto, received 581 first-preference votes. The candidate was overjoyed, saying she expected only five or six as most Travellers, including herself, couldn't register to vote without a permanent address.

Nan Joyce spent most of her life on the road. She was one of nine children born to John O'Donoghue, a horse trainer, and his wife Nan McCann. She married John Joyce when she was 16

and went on to have 11 children, who were often forced to live in appalling conditions.

She recounted living in a rat-infested camp in Priorswood in north county Dublin and losing her first grand-child Anna Marie to meningitis which, she believed, was caused by the squalid conditions. The Joyce family moved to Clondalkin and, in 1982, was forced to move again to Tallaght where some 100 families were living on the site earmarked for the Tallaght by-pass road.

Vigilante groups circled the site in an attempt to force the Travellers to move, while a number of residents marched on

Dublin County Council calling for the eviction of Travellers families. Travellers, meanwhile, responded by marching on the Dáil and went on to establish the Committee for the Rights of Travellers, jointly chaired by Nan Joyce and Tony Hackett.

It published a manifesto, calling for a minister with responsibility for Travellers who would ensure that Travellers were consulted on all development programmes.

Nan Joyce was an eloquent, passionate and tireless campaigner. She spoke at schools, universities and public gatherings all around the country, calling for equal rights for Travellers while attempting to break the barriers between Traveller and settled communities.

When she moved to Belfast, she established the Northern Ireland Council for Travelling People, inspiring a new generation to become politically active.

In 2010, President Mary McAleese presented her with a Lifetime Achievement Award for her campaigning work.

She spent her final years in Dublin and when she died in 2018, there were numerous tributes praising her for "rising above the hatred, prejudice with integrity and respect for human rights". Fellow Traveller activist Eileen Flynn described her as a history-maker and an inspiration who led the way for many Traveller women and men.

Eileen Flynn would make history herself when she became the first Traveller to sit in the Seanad in 2020. In March 2022, she became first member of the Traveller community to address the Dáil. Her mentor Nan Joyce would consider that progress, even if there is still a way to go.

CF

Nan Joyce's election manifesto, the first Traveller to run in a general election. Picture courtesy of Alan Kinsella

VOTE NO 1 ANN JOYCE

1982

Photo: Derek Speirs Report.

ANN JOYCE IS A TRAVELLER, a Mother of eleven children, a Grandmother and an Irish Citizen.

ANN JOYCE was educated for about three years at primary school in Ireland and England.

ANN JOYCE was born in Tipperary and met her husband John Joyce who is a Dublin born Traveller when she was sixteen.

ANN JOYCE IS PROUD TO BE A TRAVELLER and was selected as a candidate in Dublin South West constituency by THE COMMITTEE FOR THE RIGHTS OF TRAVELLERS of which she is a founder member.

ANN JOYCE will be CAMPAIGNING SOLELY ON THE ISSUE OF TRAVELLERS RIGHTS as contained in the Statement of Aims of the Committee for the Rights of Travellers which she helped to formulate.

ANN JOYCE is offering the decent fair minded people of Dublin South West the opportunity to use their vote in a positive way for JUSTICE, ACCEPTANCE and FAIR PLAY.

Mary Maher

(1940-2021)

Award-winning journalist, feminist and trade union activist

Mary Maher's ambition in moving to Dublin from Chicago was simple: she thought that a year abroad might give a boost to her CV and help her get a job with the *Boston Globe* newspaper.

She was given three months' probation at the *Irish Times* by News Editor Donal Foley in 1965 and was paid £15 a week. Thirty-six years later, when she retired from the newspaper, she received a 'knock-down', the noisy tribute traditionally reserved for male printers.

Mary Maher. Picture courtesy of Derek Speirs

"Mary was a true trailblazer, role model and inspiration," said President Michael D Higgins. "Her importance as an activist in the public area was accompanied by a professional commitment in journalism that broke so many ceilings, all of which advanced the causes that affected women's lives."

Mary was born in Chicago on 9 November 1940, one of Bonnie and James Maher's five children. Her paternal family were originally from Killenaule in Co Tipperary. She studied at Barat College and then worked on the society desk of the Republican-leaning *Chicago Tribune* in the early 1960s before moving to Dublin.

At the time, so-called 'women's pages' traditionally focused on cooking, shopping and homemaking and initially they held no interest for Mary. According to the anthology *Changing the Times*, she remembered how "real reporters" patronised such pages in Chicago.

But Donal Foley had different ideas. In the pub, he suggested "Women First", a page with "serious articles, scathing social attacks and biting satire". This had real appeal. For Mary, her role combined "the real reporter bit with a concentrated focus on the wrongs of women, plus useful factual information for the women whose work happened to be running a home".

Other newspapers followed her lead and, according to Mary "when the Irish Women's Liberation Movement burst upon us in 1969, the women's pages became a forum that would not otherwise have been there".

Mary was a founder member of the Irish Women's Liberation Movement and was one of the organisers of the Contraception Train protest. This took place on 22 May 1971 when 47 women took the train from Dublin to Belfast to buy contraceptives, which were not legally available at the time in the Republic.

Mary herself missed the train; she had just given birth to her second child in the National Maternity Hospital in Holles Street.

She had married Des Geraghty, who would later become President of Siptu, in 1969, and the couple had two daughters Maeve and Nóra. Although they had separated, Mary and Des later collaborated on his 1994 book about their friend, singer Luke Kelly.

Seamus Dooley of the National Union of Journalists said that Mary's career had been marked by a number of firsts, "glass-ceilings smashed by dint of hard work, determination, good humour and dedication to her union".

She was the first *Irish Times* woman to return to work after marriage and the first to get paid maternity leave. An ardent trade unionist, she became the first 'mother', or shop steward, of the chapel at the paper. In 2014, she became an NUJ Member of Honour.

Mary, who was also an author and playwright, received many awards throughout her career, including one from the National Gay Federation "for above-average journalism".

According to her friend Maeve Binchy, Mary had "the great advantage of not knowing the sacred cows and by the time she did know, she had enough courage not to care about them".

She was still singing *Bread and Roses*, the feminist anthem while a resident of Shannagh Bay Nursing Home in Bray, Co Wicklow. Mary was 81 when she died on November 30, 2021.

Paul O'Neill, editor of the *Irish Times* said Mary was among the last of an extraordinary first generation of women journalists who changed the newspaper and Irish journalism and contributed enormously to changing society. The paper has set up a bursary in her name to support aspiring journalists from under-represented backgrounds.

RW

Picture courtesy of Derek Speirs

'Mary was a true trailblazer, role model and inspiration' – President Michael D Higgins

Eavan Boland

(1944-2020)

Poet, author and acclaimed female voice in Irish literature

In the words of Eavan Boland, it is "easier to have a political murder in an Irish poem than a washing machine". However, the award-winning writer, who described herself as a feminist but not a feminist poet, made it her business to change that.

Through her poetry, she considered the experiences and identity of women, and her work had a lasting impact. "In my generation," she said, "women went from being the objects of the Irish poem to being the authors of the Irish poem."

Her lifelong friend Mary Robinson quoted from Eavan's poem *The Singers* in her inaugural address as Ireland's first female President in December 1990: "As a woman, I want the women who have felt themselves outside history to be written back into history, in the words of Eavan Boland, 'finding a voice where they found a vision'."

Eavan wrote over 10 poetry collections, as well as an award-winning essay collection and prose writings. She was also the author of an anthology of German women poets. She received the Lannan Literary Award for Poetry for her 1994 collection

Eavan Boland at the 2017 Irish Book Awards, one of many awards she received in her lifetime. Picture courtesy of Patrick Bolger

Mary Lavin and Eavan Boland.
Picture courtesy of the Irish Times

In a Time of Violence which was also shortlisted for the TS Eliot prize. The New York Times made her 2001 collection, Against Love Poetry, a Notable Book of the Year. In 2015, Irish readers included her poem Quarantine about the 1847 Famine as one of Ireland's favourite poems of the last 100 years.

Other accolades include the 2012 Pen Award for creative nonfiction for A Journey with Two Maps: Becoming a Woman Poet, her induction into the American Academy of Arts and Sciences in 2016 and, the following year, a lifetime achievement award at the Irish Book Awards.

Eavan was born in Dublin on 24 September 1944, the youngest of five children of Frances Kelly, a painter, and Frederick Boland, a diplomat. Her father was appointed as the first Irish ambassador to the United Kingdom and later took on the role of permanent representative to the United Nations.

Consequently, the family moved to London and then to New York. This was difficult for Eavan – an experience she shared in her poem An Irish Childhood in England: 1951 – and she returned to Ireland to study as a boarder at the Holy Child School in Killiney, Dublin.

Eavan was still at university in Trinity College Dublin in 1962 when her first poetry collection, 23 Poems was published. She married novelist Kevin Casey in 1969, and the couple had two daughters Sarah and Eavan. "I was a woman in a house in the suburbs, married with two small children. It was a life lived by many women around me, but it was still not named in Irish poetry."

She wanted to put the life she lived into the poems she wrote. "And I couldn't accept the possibility that the life of the woman would not, or could not, be named in the poetry of my own nation."

Marking the centenary of the admission of women to Trinity College Dublin, honorary degrees were conferred on seven women from varied walks of life, from left, the Hon Hilary M. Weston LL.D., Judge Fidelma O'Kelly Macken LL.D., Dr Shirley Ann Jackson Sc.D., Garry Hynes Litt.D., Eavan Boland Litt.D., Dame Mary Peters LL.D., Dr Alison Elliot and Chancellor of Trinity College Dublin, Dr Mary Robinson. Picture by Brenda Fitzsimons, courtesy of the *Irish Times*

was writer-in-residence at both Trinity College Dublin and University College Dublin.

In 1996, she was appointed professor of humanities, professor of English and director of the creative writing programme at Stanford University in California. She was still working there when the coronavirus pandemic struck. She returned to Dublin where she continued to teach remotely.

She died on 27 April 2020 after a stroke. Her final volume of poetry, *The Historians*, was published the same year after her death and she was posthumously awarded the Costa Book Award for poetry.

She succeeded. According to Melanie Rehak in the New York Times Book Review, Eavan's voice is "famous for its unwavering feminism as well as its devotion to both the joys of domesticity and her native Ireland".

Eavan taught at universities in Ireland and the United States and

Her work has been studied by thousands of Irish students and, according to Anne Fogarty, of the *Irish Book Review*, "modern Irish poetry would be unthinkable without her presence".

RW

Christine Buckley

(1946-2014)

Campaigner for survivors of industrial schools and those in search of their families

Remembered by her husband Donal Buckley

Christine was like a miner who was quick to spot a diamond in the rough. She could recognise people who would respond to her with resilience, and she helped a number overcome their setbacks and hardship. They include our son Darragh. She helped him overcome his dyslexia at a time when it was only beginning to be generally recognised as a widespread issue.

She also helped actor and author Glenn Gannon, who got his first taste for acting and writing for stage at the drama classes in the centre which Christine established to help survivors.

The ball really started rolling for Christine after she traced her father to Nigeria. In 1992, he came back with her to meet our family in Ireland. They both went on the *Gay Byrne Hour* radio show and she spoke about her search for her parents and her identity and about the severe regime suffered by her and other children in St Vincent's Industrial School (Goldenbridge) Inchicore, Dublin, in the 1950s and 1960s.

The response to her story, from both survivors of industrial schools and others who sought their parents, was overwhelming. And it set a challenge to seek help by way of counselling and other supports to address the trauma they suffered from the stigma of having been interned in industrial schools, the pain of family separation, or being branded as criminal or illegitimate. As a nurse and survivor, she felt obliged to apply her skills to assist fellow survivors.

Her campaign gathered momentum after Louis Lentin featured her story and those of other survivors in the 1996 TV programme *Dear Daughter*.

In April that year, Christine and another Goldenbridge survivor Carmel McDonnell-Byrne organised "One Happy Day" in the Royal Dublin Society (RDS) in Dublin. Survivors from throughout the country came together to show that they had survived, and to share their experience with other survivors. Some met survivors and siblings they hadn't seen for decades.

On 11 May 1999, then Taoiseach Bertie Ahern apologised on behalf of the State and its citizens to the victims. He announced a package of measures to address their abuse: a Commission to inquire into child abuse, The Ryan Commission, and a professional counselling service for victims. Christine played a key role in securing the apology. This subsequently led to redress for survivors.

Then Health Minister Micheál Martin also provided Christine with premises to accommodate the Aislinn Centre where survivors could meet and share their experiences with peers who understood what they had suffered. She recognised that many survivors had very poor education and she and Carmel organised literacy and art classes, and drama therapy, among other subjects, to assist them. She also encouraged survivors to attend counselling.

As well as helping survivors get housing, social welfare and other assistance, she and her team encouraged survivors to develop their talents in the creative arts, including writing, painting and acting. Peer support is also a key feature of the centre.

Thus, she spread her gift for inspiring resilience in survivors. Among those survivors were women who had also been in Magdalene laundries and mother and baby institutions.

While in her thirties, Christine herself married and had three children: Cliona, Darragh and Conor. As well as bestowing her love on them, she made sure that they got very good schooling.

In June 2009, she was one of the leaders of the March of Solidarity which saw thousands of people walk through the streets of the capital in support of survivors. That year she was also one of the winners of the People of the Year Awards.

Her volunteering work was recognised when she won Irish Volunteer of the Year and European Volunteer of the Year.

After her death, the Aislinn Centre she founded changed its name to the Christine Buckley Centre for Education & Support in recognition of her important work. Thanks to her, that work goes on.

'Christine was like a miner who was quick to spot a diamond in the rough. She could recognise people who would respond to her with resilience, and she helped a number overcome their setbacks and hardships'

Christine Buckley and her son Conor with the thousands of people who took part in a silent march in Dublin in 2009 in solidarity with survivors of sexual abuse. Picture by Colin Keegan, Collins, courtesy of Donal Buckley

Marian Finucane

(1950-2020)

Trailblazing broadcaster, feminist and charity organiser

For her husband John Clarke, she was the woman "who made the world a bit easier to live in". For the rest of us, she was the woman we listened to when we wanted to make sense of the world.

Marian Finucane's unexpected death in January 2020 shocked the country. The iconic broadcaster had had an undeniable impact.

In the words of former president Mary Robinson, Marian was "important because she was a trailblazer. She was honest. She moved agendas; she just went on blazing that trail. She wasn't afraid of Church or State".

Marian, herself, said that she had felt lucky to be part of the national conversation.

She was born in Dublin in May 1950, one of six children. Her father Daniel, who died when she was 12, was a garda sergeant, while her mother Maura was a teacher.

Although she studied architecture at the College of Technology

Marian Finucane. All pictures courtesy of RTÉ Archives

in Bolton Street, Dublin, a chance meeting at a party with RTE's John O'Donoghue changed the course of her career. She became a continuity announcer with the station.

Her big break came in May 1979 when she was appointed presenter of *Women Today*, a show focused on female issues encompassing everything from reproductive rights to employment discrimination.

The show's agenda attracted much criticism but Betty Purcell, the award-winning producer who worked alongside Marian, said that "she was brave when it was hard to be brave" and that the members of her production team always felt she had their back.

That year, she won a Jacob's Award for her work on *Women Today*. The following year, she received a Prix Italia for her documentary on one woman's journey for an abortion. Later,

she was awarded an honorary doctorate by Dublin Institute of Technology in recognition of her achievements in journalism and broadcasting.

In 1986, Marian began presenting a new phone-in radio programme called *Liveline*. She perfected the art of having an intimate conversation with a caller, one that just happened to be broadcast over the national airways.

By that stage, she and John had two children, Jack and Sinéad, but their world was shattered when eight-year-old Sinead was diagnosed with leukaemia in 1990. Marian worked on Liveline throughout Sinéad's illness, driving to the hospital after every show. John said that it was her way of coping with the knowledge that their child was dying.

After Sinéad's funeral, her mother was never able to visit her daughter's grave again.

In 1999, *The Marian Finucane Show* was launched in Gay Bryne's morning weekday slot before it moved to the weekend. She attracted some of the highest ratings on radio and some memorable interviews.

The most renowned of these took place in 2008 when Marian spoke to her close friend, the writer Nuala O'Faolain when she was dying of cancer. It was raw and unflinching and earned a place in Irish broadcasting history.

In 2015, Marian married John. By then, the two had been a couple for over 30 years. When they first met, both Marian and John were married.

Marian and architect Larry Granville had wed when she was in her early 20s. In a rare interview, Marian said that the two "got on brilliantly but we weren't a good marriage, simple as that".

Marian and John travelled extensively together, and on a visit to South Africa they saw the impact of HIV on that country. Inspired, they set up a charitable foundation, Friends in Ireland, to help vulnerable children with HIV. A 2004 documentary Marian's Journey focused on their work there.

On 2 January 2020, Marian died in her sleep in her Co Kildare home. The 69-year-old, who had suffered from a heart condition, had undiagnosed pneumonia.

In the words of historian Dr Mary McAuliffe, she was "a feminist trailblazer, a presenter and interviewer whose commitment to women's rights, equalities and voices contributed to the ongoing normalisation of women's and gender issues as important and central to Irish life, politics and society".

A year after Marian's death, a bursary fund to help women restart their education was launched in her memory.

RW

Deirdre O'Connor was an architect of conviction and a teacher with instinct. Picture courtesy of Arthur Gibney & Partners Architecture

Deirdre O'Connor

(1951-1999)

Award-winning architect and teacher

Architect Deirdre O'Connor left her work diary open on her desk for everyone at Arthur Gibney & Partners Architecture on Harcourt St in Dublin to see. It contained a simple list of key tasks for the day, all of which were ticked complete before she finished work.

Former architect colleagues offer this insight while describing a woman who was "very focused, thorough, precise, organised and with an eagle eye for design".

"We all respected Deirdre," they said, recalling their time working with the distinguished architect in the early 1990s on Gibney & Partners' Dublin City University projects.

"She required perfection on the job," they said. "She had many years of experience in the profession by then, when the number of women working in the architectural and construction industry was much lower than now. Looking back, we realise she gave us younger female architects confidence to progress with our own careers no matter what. She didn't treat us any different to our male colleagues – we just had a job to do."

Joan O'Connor, left, with her friend Deirdre. Picture courtesy of Joan O'Connor

Her design, with Ed Toovey, for the 400-seat James Larkin lecture theatre went on to win a regional award from the Royal Institute of the Architects of Ireland (RIAI) in 1992. Other distinctive commissions included renovating Dr Steevens' Hospital in Dublin, the design of Patrick Guilbaud's Michelin-starred restaurant at the Merrion Hotel and the Bookend apartment building in Temple Bar in Dublin's city centre.

She was also a member of the team that won the commission for the Irish Pavilion at the World's Fair EXPO in Seville in 1992.

Deirdre O'Connor's governing principle was that good design could lead to a better quality of life in Dublin, an idea evident in a study she wrote as Housing Research Unit scholar in 1979. *Housing in Dublin's Inner City* called on central and local governments to encourage inner city renewal.

Then, as now, there was widespread concern about the housing market and the growing division between "the housing haves and housing have nots", as the Economic Social and Research Institute warned in a report in the same year. Deirdre O'Connor said the solution was providing houses to suit all socio-economic groups.

She also co-edited, with John Graby, the Phaidon architectural guide to Dublin in 1993.

Dublin-born Deirdre O'Connor studied architecture at the College of Technology on Bolton Street, Dublin in 1968 when few women chose that career. She qualified in 1973 and in a career that was cut short by her untimely death in 1999, she won prizes, tutored at the School of Architecture in UCD, was made a fellow of the RIAI in 1988 and became the first female president of the Architectural Association of Ireland.

She was involved in much more besides, but to all her endeavours she brought her intellectual honesty and rigour, as Joan O'Connor noted in an obituary to her dear friend in the *Irish Times* in 1999. She said that Deirdre's academic and professional record should be construed against the backdrop, in time and attitude, of the profession and industry in which she worked. "While not a feminist, she was a distinctive and sometimes intimidating role model for younger women architects," she wrote.

The RIAI established the Deirdre O'Connor medal in her name in 2000, an award given to the students with the best results in the RIAI Professional Practice exam. It is a fitting tribute to a woman described as an architect of conviction and a teacher by instinct and in practice.

CF

The Bookend building on Essex Quay, Dublin, which was designed by Deirdre O'Connor. Pictures courtesy of Ros Kavanagh

'Looking back, we realise she gave us younger female architects confidence to progress with our own careers no matter what. She didn't treat us any different to our male colleagues – we just had a job to do'

Mary Raftery

(1957-2012)

Groundbreaking journalist whose work publicising child abuse changed Ireland for ever

Former colleague Fintan O'Toole described her as the most important journalist of the last 30 years. He went on to add that Mary Raftery didn't just reflect society, "she changed Ireland, significantly and for the better'".

In 1999, Mary's three-part series States of Fear shone a light on the horrific experiences of those who suffered sexual, physical and mental abuse in religious-run industrial schools. Her 2002 documentary *Cardinal Secrets* investigated clerical child sex abuse allegations in Dublin.

The programmes, shown on RTÉ, led to two commissions of inquiry. The Commissions' respective reports – Ryan in May 2009 and Murphy in November of the same year – caused a sea-change in Irish society.

"What television can do, if you get it right, is it can concentrate and focus a story at a particular time, and make people face it and make people furious," Mary said, in 2010. "So it was a question of constructing a series of programmes that wouldn't allow people to go back into denial again. In other words, that

Documentary film-maker and journalist Mary Raftery in her office in 2009. Picture courtesy of RTÉ Archives

The cover of *Suffer the Little Children*, Mary's book on the Industrial Schools

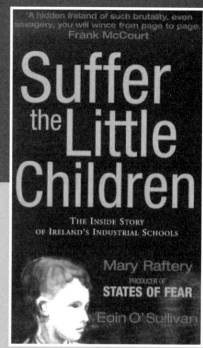

'A hidden Ireland of such brutality, even savagery, you will wince from page to page.'
Frank McCourt

Suffer the Little Children

THE INSIDE STORY
OF IRELAND'S INDUSTRIAL SCHOOLS

Mary Raftery
PRODUCER OF
STATES OF FEAR

Eoin O'Sullivan

the body of evidence would be so overwhelming that it could not be denied any more."

Mary was born on 21 December 1957, one of Adrian and Ita Raftery's four children. Adrian was a diplomat and the family lived in France when Mary was young, returning to Dublin when she was 12.

She studied engineering in University College Dublin, where she was elected education officer of the student union. The union's president at the time was David Waddell. The two would later marry and have a son Ben.

Mary had become interested in journalism while at university and she began working first for *In Dublin* magazine and then *Magill*. While there, she investigated the Dunne crime family and learned of the abuse some of them, including the drug dealer Larry Dunne, had suffered in institutions run by religious orders.

She moved to RTÉ and began working on *Today Tonight* where she broke the story that Taoiseach Charles Haughey received a payment from property developer Patrick Gallagher.

The following year, she won the first of her many awards when she was named woman journalist of the year for *Mysterious Circumstances*, a *Today Tonight* documentary on psychiatric hospitals.

Her groundbreaking series *States of Fear* led directly to then Taoiseach Bertie Ahern's public apology on behalf of the State to those who had been abused in the institutions.

The day after the Ryan Report into Church and State child abuse was released, Mary described it as "simply a devastating report... a monument to the shameful nature of Irish society through most of the decades of the twentieth century, and arguably even today".

After she left RTÉ in 2002, Mary wrote regular columns for the *Irish Times*, lectured at several institutions including Dublin City University and New York University and continued her documentary work.

She was diagnosed with ovarian cancer in 2010 and her final documentary *Behind the Walls* was produced in 2011, a two-part investigation into the history of psychiatric hospitals in Ireland.

She was just 54 when she died at St Vincent's Hospital in Dublin on 10 January 2012.

The then Archbishop of Dublin Diarmuid Martin paid tribute to her, saying that the Church was now a better place for children: "Bringing the truth out is always a positive thing, even though it may be a painful truth."

Colm O'Gorman, founder of One in Four, an organisation that supports victims of sexual abuse, said:

"She demanded attention to the stories she told. And they changed Ireland. They changed our society."

RW

RTÉ television producer and journalist Mary Raftery (left) and researcher Sheila Ahern, with some of the awards they won for their work on the RTÉ Television documentary *States of Fear*, in May 2000. Picture courtesy of RTÉ Archives

Mary Mulvihill

(1959-2015)

Pioneering science writer and broadcaster

Mary Mulvihill had a lifelong habit of making every hour of every day count. As her hero Charles Darwin said: "A man who dares to waste one hour of time has not discovered the value of life". She would have agreed, though she would certainly have added the words, 'or a woman', to the phrase.

The Mary Mulvihill Association, set up after her death, offers that vignette to describe a woman who was determined to highlight women's contribution to science. She was also "on a mission to tell everyone how ingenious Irish ideas have changed the world", as she put it.

Above, Mary looking at an orrery at an exhibition in Kilmainham, Dublin, in 2015 and, right, hillwalking in Torridon, Scotland, in 2010. Pictures courtesy of her husband Dr Brian Dolan

Her life's work was lauded by many, including Dame Jocelyn Bell Burnell, the Northern Irish astrophysicist who received the Copley Medal, the world's oldest scientific award, in 2021.

Dame Bell Burnell praised Mary's ability to hang snippets and stories on places, and enliven those places through those stories. "Geology, archaeology, sociology and technology jostle each other, producing interesting interactions," she wrote when *Ingenious Ireland* was reissued in 2019.

Mary Mulvihill said she had wanted to write a readable directory of visitor centres and was shocked, halfway through research, when she discovered it had been done before – in 1881!

"It was surely time for an update," she wrote. Her encyclopaedia of Ireland's science heritage ran to 500 pages as she added in biographies of inventors, engineers, philosophers and scientists who were either born or worked in Ireland.

Mary qualified from Trinity College Dublin with a first-class honours degree in genetics in 1981. She returned to complete a Master's in statistics followed, in 1988, by a diploma in journalism from Dublin City University.

She wrote regularly for the *Irish Times*, edited and contributed to Enterprise Ireland's bi-monthly publication *Technology Ireland* and also worked as a broadcaster. She hosted her own science programmes on RTE Radio 1 and Lyric FM.

'She was on a mission to tell everyone how ingenious Irish ideas have changed the world'

Above, Mary with a culm crusher, or grinding stone, on the river Barrow in 2013 and, right, looking at a ring-marked stone near Glenbeigh, Kerry, in 2012). Pictures courtesy of her husband, Dr Brian Dolan

Inspired by her radio work, she led guided tours through her hometown of Dublin. She produced podcasts celebrating the city's Botanic Gardens, the Hill of Tara in Meath and the Barrow River, among many others.

In 1990, Mary founded Women in Technology and Science (WITS) to actively promote women in technology and science in Ireland. She later edited two collections of biographical essays on Irish women scientists and pioneers – *Stars, Shells and Bluebells* (1997) and *Lab Coats and Lace* (2009).

In 2002-2003, her work was acknowledged when she won the Irish National Science and Technology Journalist of the Year award.

On International Women's Day in 2015, she led the walk she had initiated the previous year to mark the naming of the Rosie Hackett Bridge (see entry on Rosie Hackett) in Dublin. She died only a few months later on 12 June aged just 55. But the memory of this writer, broadcaster, commentator and tour guide lives on.

In 2016, friends and family set up the Mary Mulvihill Association and established an award in her name to celebrate her work and to promote her legacy.

She received a posthumous honour for outstanding achievement in Societal Impact from Dublin City University in 2020. A year later, her life and work were commemorated with a plaque at her former home in Stoneybatter, Dublin. Her light shines on.

RW

Mary and a giant tortoise in the Galapagos in 2011.
Picture courtesy of Dr Brian Dolan

Maria Place

(1967-2021)

Artist, activist, author
– a modern Renaissance woman

Maria Place loved her home of Ballymun on Dublin's north side. She was raised in the city suburb and spent much of her time living and working in the community. Throughout her life, this creative and artistic woman worked hard to improve the lives of the people around her.

Her mantra was "if not me, then who?" and it was one that she followed to the letter. She had an open and non-judgmental approach, which appealed to people, and she viewed every project she worked on as a collaboration.

Her love of music and song developed as a child. Maria adored musical theatre and showtunes. She performed in church choirs, folk bands rock groups and wrote many of her own songs.

Along with one of her oldest friends, Krystel Harris, she was a member of the Coconuts Trio in *The Commitments*, the 1991 film version of Roddy Doyle's novel. According to her beloved sister Jennie, she never lived it down.

Maria Place: 'an inspirational figure to all who came into her light' - Mark O'Brien, director of Axis
All pictures courtesy of her family

Maria at work with Ballymun Local Drugs & Alcohol Task Force

Later she used this experience to good effect, setting up the Ballymun East Young Entertainers in the early 1990s. She produced and directed three community shows called *Celebrate!* in Ballymun's Axis Art Centre and Theatre, which involved several different community groups and organisations participating in a variety show format.

Maria, who was born on 18 January 1967, was one of 11 children. Her family was an extremely close-knit one.

She studied journalism in Dublin City University as a mature student. She had already gained much practical experience when she and Krystel set up a local and short-lived newspaper called *SubCity Times* in the late 1980s. She passionately believed in the value of communities telling and owning their own stories. Her journalism training came to the fore when she later self-published two books.

Maria, a community development consultant, worked for Fingal County Council, Ballymun Regional Youth Resource Centre, Ballymun Whitehall Area Partnership and Ballymun Job Centre. She was also involved in learning and development for Tusla.

She spoke fluent French and put her expertise to good use while she was in Strasbourg working with the Council of Europe on a research project.

In addition, she was instrumental in the creation of many long-lasting projects in the local area, including the Axis, Ballymun Regional Youth Resource (which she managed in 2012) and the Togail Housing Co-op, as well as other affordable housing in the Ballymun and Finglas communities.

Maria played a key role in the Ballymun Local Drugs Task Force, which she chaired during 2007 and 2009. Her dedication to volunteering was publicly recognised when she received an award from the City of Dublin Youth Services Board.

'Her mantra was "if not me, then who?" and it was one that she followed to the letter'

Maria Place speaking at the Ballymun Regional Youth Resource with programme manager Donnacadh Hurley. Picture courtesy of her family

Despite her many commitments, Maria managed to find time to achieve an MPhil in Psychoanalysis from Trinity College Dublin in 2012. Afterwards, she attended Ballyfermot College of Further Education and completed a Higher National Diploma in Fibre Art in 2016. Her creation of wearable fibre was modelled and presented in a collaborative sculptural piece in the National Botanic Gardens Sculpture in Context exhibition.

A community activist, youth officer, artist, author, singer and dancer, Maria dedicated her life to building a better and brighter future for her local community. Her sister Jennie said that "she understood the value of civic engagement, treating people with genuine compassion and care, and lived a life anchored in community values and meaningful dialogue".

After a diagnosis of cancer, she passed away at home in the housing estate she was instrumental in building, on 17 January 2021, the day before her 54th birthday. Her mother Kay and her daughter Jessica were by her side.

She had dedicated her college dissertation to her daughter, saying "To Jessica, thank you for being born. Without you, I would be here, there and everywhere."

Her sister Jennie says that being a mother inspired Maria to want to change the world. And she did her best to do so. Maria was, in the words of Mark O'Brien, director of Axis, "an inspirational figure to all who came into her light".

RW

Dr Aoibheann Gaughran

(1975-2021)

Zoologist, groundbreaking badger researcher, communicator and teacher

Remembered by friend and colleague Dr John M. Rochford

An enthusiastic naturalist from a very early age, Aoibheann came to the formal study of natural science and zoology later than some. She had already established a career in marketing before she applied to study Science at Trinity College Dublin (TCD) as a mature student, entering first year in 2009.

Right from the start, it was evident she was on track for great things: she came first in biology in her first year; she was successful at the Foundation Scholarship examinations in her second year, and was awarded the prestigious Gold Medal for "showing exceptional merit" in her final zoology exams.

By this time, it was clear that Aoibheann was 'hooked on mammals'. An enthusiast for the outdoors, fieldwork was her passion. She never turned down the opportunity to be out in the field, studying, monitoring and recording, whether it was birds, bats or bees.

Or pets. She did a stint at Dogs Aid in 2013, describing herself as "a cat herder, pooper scooper and belly tickler". The following year, she found time to sort skeletons at the Zoology Museum at TCD.

Dr Aoibheann Gaughran. Picture courtesy of Trinity College Dublin

She returned to Zoology in 2014 to start what turned out to be an extraordinary study of badgers in Co Wicklow, which earned her a PhD in 2018. Although initially daunted by the challenge ("Is there really anything new to be discovered about such a well-studied species?" she thought), through the painstaking analysis of data obtained from GPS tracking of the animals, she made a major breakthrough in the understanding of their ranging behaviour.

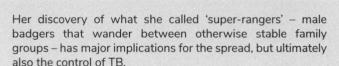

Her discovery of what she called 'super-rangers' – male badgers that wander between otherwise stable family groups – has major implications for the spread, but ultimately also the control of TB.

Throughout her time as a graduate student, Aoibheann contributed hugely to the research and teaching ethos of the department. She was a natural communicator, teacher and organiser. She was always ready to offer support and advice to other students (and staff) and always eager to discover new things and learn new skills. She was the epitome of the 'life-long learner'.

Having obtained her PhD, Aoibheann joined the staff of Zoology as a Research Fellow and, following some further work on her beloved badgers and a season's fieldwork on the

Dr Aoibheann Gaughran and Prof Jane Stout with President Michael D. Higgins in the grounds of Áras an Uachtaráin. Pictures courtesy of Tony Maxwell/Áras an Uachtaráin

ecology of the Wild Atlantic Way, she coordinated a year-long biodiversity audit of the grounds of Áras an Uachtaráin. It was commissioned by President Michael D Higgins with a view to managing the area for nature conservation.

In 2021, she began work on a four-year Nature+Energy project, funded by Science Foundation Ireland, aimed at maximising the positive impact of wind farms on biodiversity.

Despite the intensity of this work, Aoibheann still managed to stay involved with numerous other biodiversity initiatives, one of which was to replicate the work carried out at the Áras at Trinity College. Her enthusiasm knew no bounds.

Aoibheann's sudden and untimely death, just as she was really establishing herself in her field, has left a gap that will not be easily filled. Her many colleagues and friends paid tribute to a woman whose positivity, energy and sheer passion for her work inspired all who came in contact with her – students, fellow researchers and academics alike.

Plans are being developed to honour her legacy with an award for student field studies.

'Her discovery of what she called 'super-rangers' – male badgers that wander between otherwise stable family groups – has major implications for the spread, but ultimately also the control of TB'

Jemma Redmond

(1978-2016)

Pioneering scientist and biotechnologist who 3D-printed living cells

Jemma Redmond, CEO of the bioprinting start-up company Ourobotics, was the first person to build a bioprinter that could 3D-print human cells and keep them alive. "We make robots that make people," she used to say, describing her pioneering work in pushing the boundaries of what was possible in tissue engineering.

Her vision was to use that process to 3D-print human organs that could be transplanted by surgeons into the human body. She estimated that hospitals would be able to buy reasonably priced bioprinters capable of 3D-printing organs within 20 years. It would eliminate the need to put people on organ-donor waiting lists and cut tens of thousands of euro off the cost, she said.

It sounded like science-fiction – she said so herself – but, in her lifetime, Jemma Redmond won several awards and attracted global attention for her innovations. In 2015, she designed and built the first 10-material bioprinter capable of using live human cells.

In 2015, Jemma designed and built the first 10-material bioprinter capable of using live human cells

She and her team had spent four intense months in China building a prototype with support from the HAX accelerator programme, a scheme that helps start-ups take steps towards commercialisation. When complete, they flew to Los Angeles to give a demonstration at a conference. Jemma, jet-lagged and exhausted, accidently leaned on the display table, sending the bioprinter, named Revolution, crashing to the floor.

"The room went silent," she recalled. "I just kicked the machine under the table... it was grand. We came back to Cork and built another machine and went a bit further."

In Ireland, she returned to her laboratory space at Summerhill North in Cork city and worked on, showing the kind of resilience that won her widespread praise. Colleagues spoke of a woman whose remorseless logic, brilliance and all-encompassing knowledge overcame obstacles, or at least figured out a way around them.

She had come to the field of bioprinting when she found out that she could not have children. She was born intersex – "I have some differences in my body," as she explained it – and

253

set about using her expertise to 'fix it'. She believed that she could 3D-print ovaries and a womb and, in doing so, help many others with fertility problems.

Born in Tallaght, Co Dublin, in 1978, she was the eldest of Lorraine and Christy Cahill's three children. She was building prototypes from an early age, taking apart everyday appliances – cookers, heaters, whatever was to hand – to see how they worked and how she might improve on the design.

She studied electronic engineering in Dublin followed by applied physics at Robert Gordon University in Aberdeen in 2000 and later completed a Master's in nano bioscience. She worked as a research assistant at University College Dublin before setting up her own company.

Jemma used her grandmother's surname 'Redmond' as the two were very close.

When she died suddenly, aged 38, friends and colleagues said she was a world leader in her field and a true innovator who saw possibilities where others didn't. Though she faced many struggles too. She had to fight for investment, funding and recognition. She posted regularly on social media about the difficulties of being intersex, calling out street harassment, verbal and physical abuse.

During her lifetime, she had to move away from her home city to find support and funding for her pioneering work. Now, at least, Dublin is belatedly honouring her significant contribution.

CF

Jemma had several qualifications but here she was trying on a mortar board for fun.

Pictures courtesy of Jemma Redmond's family.